Nancy Cooper

$2 00

P9-DXO-573

SUPPERS
AND
SNACKS

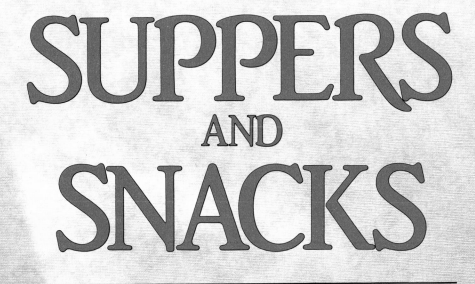

SUPPERS
AND
SNACKS

Carol Bowen

CONTENTS

Introduction 6

Sandwiches & Broiled Dishes 10

From the Pantry 22

Salads, Pastries & Pâtés 34

Special Suppers 48

One-Dish Meals 64

Index 80

ANOTHER BEST-SELLING VOLUME FROM HPBooks®
Publisher: Rick Bailey; Editorial Director: Elaine R. Woodard
Editor: Jeanette P. Egan; Art Director: Don Burton
Book Assembly: Leslie Sinclair
Typography: Cindy Coatsworth, Michelle Claridge
Book Manufacture: Anthony B. Narducci
Recipe testing by International Cookbook Services: Barbara Bloch,
President; Rita Barrett, Director of Testing

Published by HPBooks, Inc.
P.O. Box 5367, Tucson, AZ 85703 602/888-2150
ISBN 0-89586-345-6
Library of Congress Catalog Card Number 85-60085
© 1985 HPBooks, Inc. Printed in the U.S.A.
1st Printing

Originally published as Suppers and Snacks
© 1984 Hennerwood Publications Limited

Cover Photo: Clockwise from left: Beef & Cheese Rolls, Smorrebrod,
Spicy Club Sandwich, pages 14 and 15

Notice: The information contained in this book is true and complete to the best of our knowledge. All recommendations are made without any guarantees on the part of the author or HPBooks. The author and publisher disclaim all liability in connection with the use of this information.

Introduction

In order to eat well, it is not necessary to spend hours in the kitchen. Even during the week, it is possible to prepare delicious meals and snacks. Today there are several labor-saving pieces of equipment, convenience-style foods and many beautiful styles of freezer-to-oven-to-table cookware that save on valuable cleanup time. It is possible to have delicious, home-cooked meals in a fraction of the time it used to take. For this book, recipes were chosen that are delicious, nutritious and easy to prepare. With these goals in mind, you'll see that the preparation time in each of these recipes is kept to a minimum.

Preparing quick, tasty and nutritious suppers and snacks does not necessarily demand a large supply of frozen, dried or canned convenience foods. Just the opposite, it involves judiciously using a few convenience foods with fresh ingredients to save time, add flavor or reduce the workload. A well-stocked, but not heavily-stocked pantry, can prove to be a lifesaver when unexpected guests call, when a meal for four suddenly has to expand to serve six and when quick, but interesting, snacks are required.

Foods to have on hand fall into three main categories: dried and packaged products, canned goods and those foods that must be refrigerated or frozen.

DRIED & PACKAGED PRODUCTS

Keep a wide variety of dried herbs, spices and seasonings on hand. They can literally lift a dish from the ordinary to the luxury class. Remember to keep your supply fresh. If your herbs and spices are several months old, you might want to replace them. Bouillon cubes are helpful, especially if you haven't the time to make stock. Remember that bouillon cubes are salted; make adjustments in your recipe.

A good selection of dried fruits and nuts will always come in handy. They can be used as basic ingredients, or as garnishes to add an interesting touch. Currants, raisins, walnuts, almonds and pecans are a good selection to have on hand. If nuts are not used quickly, store them in the refrigerator or freezer. This prevents the fats they contain from becoming rancid and giving the nuts an off flavor.

A well-stocked pantry will also include a good selection of rice, hot and cold cereals, flour, pasta, cornmeal, sugar and other ingredients for baking. Choose a few quick mixes for breads, cakes or brownies. A package of nonfat dried milk will be useful for emergencies. A favorite dried-soup mix, sauce mix or seasoning packet may be one of your standbys. Beyond that, the choice is yours. Dried vegetables, such as onions, instant potatoes, dried peas and dried beans, keep well and are useful. A pressure cooker will save time when cooking dried peas and beans.

CANNED GOODS

These can really be a bonus when time is short. Include a good selection of condensed soups, chicken stock and beef stock. Canned stocks are excellent substitutes for homemade stock when time is short.

A few cans of fish and shellfish, such as sardines, anchovies, crab, shrimp, mussels and tuna, should be on hand. These are useful in hors d'oeuvres, salads, soups, or gratin-type dishes. Canned pâté, ham, corned beef and chicken are indispensable for a quick meal or snack. In addition to canned seafood and meats, canned vegetables and fruits, such as beans, corn, mushrooms, apricots, pears and peaches, all have a well-earned place. Don't forget canned milk for soups and sauces.

Without question, one of the most useful groups of canned goods is the wide array of tomato products, such as canned tomatoes, tomato paste and tomato sauce. These are always in season and do not have to be peeled or chopped.

Remember to keep a supply of special ingredients, such as olives, capers, chutneys or pickles. These can be used to add flavor and as garnishes. Keep a supply of sweets—for example, jams, syrups and dessert sauces.

A good selection of oils, vinegars and salad dressings will make serving a variety of salads easier. Of course, wines, spirits and liqueurs add a flavor all their own. Use the same wine for cooking that you do for drinking.

REFRIGERATED & FROZEN FOODS

A refrigerator and freezer are high on the list of kitchen essentials. A refrigerator can be stocked with eggs; milk; butter or margarine; bacon; a selection of hard and soft cheeses; a carton or two of fruit juice; a few fresh oranges, lemons and other fruits and milk.

The range of prepared foods that is available in the supermarket is extensive, and the choice of which to buy is an individual one. However, there are some foods particularly useful for preparing recipes in this book. These include frozen fish and shellfish, a good-quality ground beef, cut-up chicken and ready-made beef patties. In addition, include a good selection of home- or commercially-frozen vegetables and fruits.

In the pastry section, some ready-made crepes stacked between foil or freezer paper and frozen puff pastry will be timesavers. These will simplify meal planning and preparation.

For quick desserts, one or two favorite dessert sauces, some ice cream, frozen cakes or cookies will add the finishing touch to a meal.

Other items to keep on hand, if space permits, are lemon peel, lemon juice and chopped herbs. Store only those items you use regularly. Inventory your refrigerator and freezer on a regular basis to determine what needs to be used.

When cooking food that is to be frozen, reheating prepared dishes, or defrosting frozen foods, it is important to

Some foods to have on hand

follow food-safety rules. Remember that freezing does not destroy bacteria in foods. When the food is thawed, any bacteria that is present will start to grow again. Some foods, such as poultry, pork, sausage and shellfish, need to be handled with care since these are more susceptible to spoilage. Leftovers should always be stored in the refrigerator and not at room temperature. Most frozen foods should be thawed in the refrigerator rather than at room temperature. When reheating foods that have been made ahead or frozen, reheat thoroughly. Use most leftovers within 24 hours. If in doubt about the freshness of a food, do not eat it.

A NUTRITIOUS EATING PLAN

If snacks are planned that provide part of the daily nutrient requirements, eating snacks need not play havoc with good eating habits. A balanced and varied diet should provide all the nutrients needed for health. Eating a healthy diet does not mean buying expensive foods from health-food stores. The supermarket is the source for ingredients used in this book. These recipes have been developed so that you can choose a varied and nutritious range of foods. They can be part of a sensible overall eating plan. Current nutritional recommendations on which to base your plan include:

1. Eating lean cuts of meat and trimming away fat before cooking.
2. Eating more fish and poultry.
3. Eating less than five eggs per week. This reduces cholesterol intake.
4. Replacing high-fat foods with low-fat alternatives.

For example, substitute skimmed milk for whole milk or low-fat cheeses for high-fat cheeses.
5. Eating a wide selection of fruit and vegetables. Eat at least 4 servings daily.
6. Eating more cereals, especially whole-grain varieties.
7. Cutting down on all fats.
8. Trying to eat less salt and refined sugar.

HELPFUL EQUIPMENT

Most cooks have a favorite kitchen appliance they would not live without. It may fit in well with their lifestyle by speeding up food preparation, cooking quickly or cutting down or dispensing with time-consuming tasks. Although not essential for preparing these recipes, the appliances discussed below are especially appropriate to cooking suppers and snacks.

Mixers, Blenders & Food Processors—It is hard to remember the time when cream was whipped by hand or when cheese had to be grated by hand, endangering the knuckles. Fruit and vegetables are no longer pureed with a wooden spoon and sieve. Since the introduction of mixers, blenders and food processors, all these can be done by machine. Some of the more sophisticated models slice salad vegetables, shred vegetables, stuff sausages, and make pasta, bread and pastry.

Countertop Cooking Equipment—These ingenious countertop appliances include countertop ovens, waffle irons, griddles and toasters. They have a variety of uses that defies their size. Not only will they broil steaks, kabobs and fish, but also toast sandwiches. They can bake pizzas, pies, biscuits, cookies, pancakes, crepes and waffles. Or,

they can cook hamburgers, bacon, chops and chicken. For best results, always follow the manufacturer's instructions.
Microwave Ovens—A microwave oven is a versatile appliance for the busy cook. It cooks suppers and snacks quickly and efficiently. It cooks in minutes rather than hours, defrosts foods quickly and reheats leftovers. Many of your favorite recipes can be adapted for microwave cooking. Always follow the manufacturer's instructions.

HELPFUL HINTS

Despite the help of convenience foods and modern equipment, there are still moments in a cook's life when there is simply not enough time. However, there are some helpful ideas that the cook can use for spicing up the simplest meals so that they need never become humdrum. These include:

● Add flavor to a stuffing mix, if you don't have time to make one from scratch, by adding herbs and substituting fruit juice for half of the water. Good flavor combinations include sage and onion with apple juice or orange juice and thyme and lemon with grapefruit juice.

● Add a spoonful of cream to a sauce or to pan juices to produce that swirl of luxury on sautéed or broiled foods.

● Make delicious and unusual short-crust pastry by adding additional ingredients. Good ones to try include chopped nuts, grated fruit peels, ground spices, dried leaf herbs, wheat germ, chopped cooked bacon, cooked chopped onion, dried coconut and fruit juices, depending on whether the crust is for a sweet or savory pie.

● Savory rice dishes taste all the more delicious if you substitute fruit juice or stock for some of the cooking water. *Coconut Rice* also makes a delicious accompaniment to a curry or spiced dish. Add approximately 2 tablespoons cream of coconut to 1-1/4 cups rice; cook in the usual way.

● A good choice of marinades helps tenderize and adds flavor to economical meat cuts prior to cooking. Use this *Meat Marinade* for kabob cubes or man-size pot roasts. In a medium bowl, combine 2 tablespoons vinegar, 1 tablespoon olive oil, 1/2 teaspoon honey, 1/2 teaspoon dried leaf marjoram and 1/4 cup apple juice. Add meat; marinate at least 4 hours. Or, cover and refrigerate overnight.

● Make traditional stews and casseroles extra special by adding flavored dumplings 20 minutes before the end of the cooking time. Fruit, herb, spice or bacon-flavored dumplings are favorites. Or, top a stew or casserole with savory biscuits or choux buns for a hearty one-dish meal.

● Baste grilled meats with a flavorful mixture during cooking. Try these barbecue, mustard or marmalade sauces for enviable results.

Mustard Sauce: In a small bowl, combine 1 tablespoon wine vinegar, 1 tablespoon prepared mustard and 1/2 cup packed brown sugar.

Barbecue Sauce: In a small bowl, combine 1 tablespoon prepared mustard, 2 teaspoons brown sugar, 1 tablespoon wine vinegar and 1 tablespoon ketchup.

Marmalade Sauce: In a small bowl, combine 2 tablespoons marmalade, 2 teaspoons soy sauce and 1 tablespoon orange juice.

● Keep flavored butters in the refrigerator or freezer for topping broiled or sautéed meats and fish, and poached fish. Use flavored butters to top baked potatoes and sandwiches. Herbs, such as parsley, chives, thyme and tarragon, are versatile, or try onion butter, blue-cheese butter, mint butter and lemon butter.

● Salads needn't be made of only lettuce, tomato and cucumber. Combine an imaginative selection of everyday, as well as exotic, fruits and vegetables with fish, meats, eggs, cheese and, more importantly, a tasty dressing. Keep a variety of salad dressings on hand. Store in the refrigerator, and simply shake to use.

● Basic mayonnaise can be flavored with curry, mint, lemon, garlic or chilies for interesting additions to salads and sandwiches.

● Canned and packaged soups offer tremendous advantages to the busy cook. Use them instead of stock for stews, casseroles, chowders and sauces. Or, add cream, sherry, herbs or a topping of croutons, onion rings or paprika for a quick, flavorful soup.

GARNISHES

Remember to serve food with style by adding attractive garnishes and table settings. Mix and match foods with the following garnish ideas.

● Chopped herbs or herb sprigs
● Tomato slices or hard-cooked-egg slices
● Lemon slices, twists, butterflies or wedges
● Cucumber slices
● A dusting of spices or coconut
● Chopped, halved or whole nuts, olives, or dried fruit
● A border of shredded lettuce or Chinese cabbage
● Crispy croutons
● A golden-brown border of piped, then broiled, mashed potatoes
● A spoonful or swirl of sour cream, whipped cream or yogurt
● An aspic glaze with colorful vegetable pieces
● Hollowed-out fruit and vegetable shells
● Toasted French bread, baked choux buns or freshly cooked fluffy dumplings
● Shredded cheese or toasted bread crumbs
● Toast fingers or triangles
● Green-onion curls, carrot scrolls or decorative vegetable shapes for an Oriental effect
● Pleated and grilled bacon slices, page 63
● Julienne strips of fruit peel, such as orange, lemon or lime

Garnishes

Sandwiches & Broiled Dishes

Pork, Beef & Chicken Saté

12 oz. lean boneless pork
12 oz. beef round steak
12 oz. boneless chicken breasts, skinned
6 tablespoons vegetable oil
6 tablespoons soy sauce
1 garlic clove, crushed
1 tablespoon curry powder
1-1/2 tablespoons sugar

Peanut Sauce:
2 tablespoons vegetable oil
1 onion, finely chopped
1 garlic clove, crushed
1 teaspoon chili powder
1 teaspoon ground coriander
1/4 teaspoon ground cumin
1/2 cup peanut butter
1 cup coconut milk or chicken stock
2 tablespoons light-brown sugar
1 tablespoon soy sauce
1 tablespoon lemon juice

1. Cut pork, beef and chicken into 1/2-inch cubes; place each meat in a separate medium, glass or stainless-steel bowl.
2. In another medium bowl, combine oil, soy sauce, garlic, curry powder and sugar. Pour 1/3 of marinade over each meat. Cover and refrigerate at least 4 hours or up to 24 hours.
3. Preheat broiler. To make sauce, heat oil in a medium saucepan. Stir in onion, garlic, chili powder, coriander and cumin; cook 2 minutes. Stir in peanut butter, coconut milk or stock, brown sugar, soy sauce and lemon juice. Bring to a boil. Reduce heat; Simmer 10 minutes or until creamy. Set aside to cool.
4. Thread marinated meats on 12 small skewers, using 4 for each type of meat. If using wooden skewers, soak in cold water 30 minutes before using. Brush kabobs with a little peanut sauce. Place on a broiler-pan rack.
5. Broil under preheated broiler 6 to 8 minutes or until browned on all sides. Pork should be well-done. Serve hot with remaining peanut sauce. Makes 4 servings.

Greek Pita-Pocket Sandwiches

4 pita-bread rounds
Greek Salad
1 cup finely chopped cooked lamb
2 oz. mushrooms, thinly sliced (about 1 cup)
1 small bunch green onions, chopped
2 lettuce leaves, shredded
2 tomatoes, peeled, seeded, chopped
4 black olives, pitted, sliced
2 to 3 tablespoons plain yogurt
Salt
Freshly ground pepper
3/4 cup shredded Monterey Jack cheese (3 oz.)

1. Preheat broiler. Cut off 1 to 2 inches from top of each pita round. Carefully open to form a pocket.
2. To make Greek Salad, in a medium bowl, combine lamb, mushrooms, green onions, lettuce, tomatoes, olives, yogurt, salt and pepper.
3. Spoon Greek Salad into pita pockets. Place filled sandwiches on a baking sheet. Sprinkle cheese on sandwiches.
4. Broil under preheated broiler 5 to 6 minutes or until cheese melts. Serve immediately. Makes 4 servings.

Variation
West Indies Pita-Pocket Sandwiches: In a medium bowl, combine 1/2 cup diced cooked chicken, 1/4 cup finely chopped pineapple, 1/4 cup finely chopped green bell pepper, 1 small sliced banana, 1/4 cup chopped toasted almonds, 2 to 3 tablespoons mayonnaise, salt and freshly ground black pepper. Use to fill pita rounds.

Top to bottom: Greek Pita-Pocket Sandwiches; Pork, Beef & Chicken Saté with Peanut Sauce

Salami & Mozzarella Snacks

4 thick homemade-style bread slices
4 oz. salami, thinly sliced
4 tomatoes, peeled, sliced
Freshly ground black pepper
1 green or yellow bell pepper, sliced
8 thin mozzarella-cheese slices
1/2 teaspoon Italian seasoning

To garnish:
4 to 8 small black olives
Parsley sprigs

1. Preheat broiler. Place bread on a broiler-pan rack. Toast on 1 side under preheated broiler.
2. Turn bread slices over; cover with salami and tomatoes. Season with black pepper. Top with bell pepper and cheese. Sprinkle each with 1/8 teaspoon Italian seasoning.
3. Broil under preheated broiler about 10 minutes or until cheese melts.
4. Top with olives; garnish with parsley. Serve hot. Makes 4 servings.

Left to right: Salami & Mozzarella Snacks, Bean & Egg Snacks, Baked Ham & Cheese Loaf

Bean & Egg Snacks

1 (1-lb.) can pork and beans with tomato sauce
1 to 2 teaspoons chili powder
1 canned pimento, finely chopped
1/2 teaspoon Worcestershire sauce
1/4 cup butter or margarine
6 eggs, beaten
Salt
Freshly ground pepper
4 slices hot buttered toast
1 tomato, thinly sliced

To garnish:
Cilantro sprigs

1. In a medium saucepan, combine beans, chili powder, pimento and Worcestershire sauce. Stir over medium heat until hot.
2. Melt butter or margarine in a large skillet. Add eggs, salt and pepper. Cook over low heat until lightly scrambled.
3. Spoon scrambled eggs around edges of toast; see photo.
4. Spoon bean mixture into center of eggs. Top with tomato slices; garnish with cilantro. Serve immediately. Makes 4 servings.

Baked Ham & Cheese Loaf

1 large French-bread loaf
1/4 cup butter or margarine, room temperature
1 garlic clove, crushed
8 slices Monterey Jack cheese
8 cooked ham slices
8 salami-with-peppercorns slices
2 tomatoes, thinly sliced

1. Preheat oven to 375F (190C). Make 8 diagonal cuts at equal distances along length of loaf, cutting almost through loaf.
2. In a small bowl, cream butter or margarine and garlic; spread on cut sides of bread. Place buttered bread on a piece of foil large enough to completely wrap it.
3. Place 1 slice each of cheese, ham, salami and tomato in each cut. Press gently together to re-form loaf. Wrap loaf loosely with foil.
4. Bake in preheated oven 10 to 15 minutes.
5. Open top of foil; bake 5 minutes or until cheese melts. Pull apart or cut between filled sections to serve. Makes 4 servings.

1/Spread creamed garlic butter or margarine on cut sides of bread.

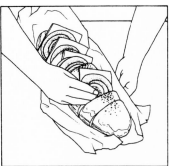

2/Place 1 slice each of cheese, ham, salami and tomato in each cut.

Smorrebrod

4 pumpernickel-bread slices
1/4 cup butter or margarine, room temperature
4 lettuce leaves
4 salami slices
2 tablespoons grated cabbage
1 tablespoon grated carrot
2 green onions, finely chopped
4 hard-cooked eggs, chopped
1/4 cup mayonnaise
Salt
Freshly ground pepper
1 teaspoon capers
1 bratwurst, broiled, sliced
1 teaspoon mango chutney
1 teaspoon chopped raisins
1 tomato, sliced
2 tablespoons radish sprouts

To serve more people, double or triple this recipe.

1. Spread bread generously with butter or margarine; top each slice with a lettuce leaf.
2. Top 2 bread slices with 2 salami slices each. In a medium bowl, combine cabbage, carrot, green onions, 2 hard-cooked eggs, 2 tablespoons mayonnaise, salt and pepper. Spoon mixture on top of salami; garnish with capers.
3. Top remaining 2 bread slices with bratwurst. In a medium bowl, combine remaining 2 hard-cooked eggs with remaining 2 tablespoons mayonnaise, chutney, raisins, salt and pepper. Spoon mixture on bratwurst. Arrange slices of tomato over chutney-egg mixture. Garnish with radish sprouts.
4. Serve 1 salami sandwich and 1 sausage sandwich per person. Makes 2 servings.

Spicy Club Sandwiches

1/2 cup diced cooked chicken
1/4 cup mayonnaise
1 teaspoon mild curry powder
1 tablespoon raisins
4 Canadian-bacon slices
8 whole-wheat-bread slices, crusts removed, toasted
4 white-bread slices, crusts removed, toasted
1/4 cup butter or margarine, room temperature
4 lettuce leaves
About 16 thin cucumber slices
1 small green bell pepper, sliced
2 tomatoes, thinly sliced
1 tablespoon chopped fresh parsley

---

1. In a medium bowl, combine chicken, mayonnaise, curry powder and raisins.
2. Cook bacon in a medium skillet over low heat until hot. Keep warm.
3. Spread 1 side of whole-wheat bread and both sides of white bread with butter or margarine.
4. Spread chicken mixture over buttered sides of 4 whole-wheat-bread slices. Top each with a buttered white-bread slice.
5. Cover each white-bread slice with a lettuce leaf, 4 cucumber slices and 1/4 of bell pepper.
6. Top each sandwich with a final whole-wheat-bread slice, buttered-side down. Cover with tomato slices and a bacon slice. Sprinkle tomato with chopped parsley. Serve immediately with a knife and fork. Makes 4 servings.

New Yorkers

8 rye-bread slices
1 (8-oz.) pkg. cream cheese, room temperature
4 smoked-salmon slices
1 red onion, sliced into rings
16 fresh parsley sprigs
Freshly ground pepper

---

1. Spread bread generously with cream cheese.
2. Cut each salmon slice in half; roll each half into a small cornet. Place a salmon cornet on top of each bread slice.
3. Top salmon with a few onion rings and 2 parsley sprigs. Sprinkle with a little pepper. Makes 4 servings.

Clockwise from left: Beef & Cheese Roll, Smorrebrod,
Spicy Club Sandwich

Beef & Cheese Rolls

4 large soft sesame rolls
6 tablespoons butter or margarine, room temperature
1/2 cup finely chopped cold roast beef
1/4 cup mayonnaise
1 tablespoon chopped fresh chives
1 to 2 teaspoons prepared horseradish
4 lettuce leaves
4 oz. sharp Cheddar cheese, thinly sliced
1 tomato, thinly sliced
2 tablespoons chutney
1 medium leek, white part only, thinly sliced
1 teaspoon grated lemon peel
1 tablespoon raisins

1. Cut 3 horizontal slits in each roll, cutting almost completely through. Spread bread layers with butter or margarine.
2. In a medium bowl, combine beef, 1/2 of mayonnaise, chives and horseradish to taste.
3. Place a lettuce leaf on bottom layer of each buttered roll; top each lettuce leaf with 1/4 of beef filling.
4. Fill middle layer of rolls with cheese, tomato and chutney.
5. Separate sliced leek into rings. In a small bowl, combine leek, lemon peel, remaining 2 tablespoons mayonnaise and raisins. Use to fill top layer of rolls. Press top of each roll down lightly before serving. Makes 4 servings.

Bacon & Cheese Sandwiches

8 thin white-bread slices, crusts removed
1 to 2 teaspoons prepared coarse mustard
4 oz. Gruyère cheese, sliced
8 bacon slices, crisp-cooked
2 tomatoes, thinly sliced
3 tablespoons butter or margarine, melted

1. Preheat oven to 450F (230C). Spread 1/2 of bread slices with mustard to taste. Top each with an equal amount of cheese, bacon and tomato slices. Cover with remaining bread slices, pressing down well.
2. Place sandwiches on a baking sheet; brush tops lightly with about 1/2 of butter or margarine.
3. Bake in preheated oven about 5 minutes or until lightly browned.
4. Using a spatula, turn sandwiches over; brush with remaining butter or margarine. Bake 3 to 5 minutes or until lightly browned. Cut diagonally in half to serve. Makes 4 servings.

French-Bread Pizzas

1 large French-bread loaf
3 tablespoons tomato paste
1 (8-oz.) can tomatoes, drained, chopped
1 teaspoon dried leaf oregano or dried leaf marjoram
Salt
Freshly ground pepper
1 cup shredded mozzarella cheese (4 oz.)
2 (2-oz.) cans anchovy fillets in oil, drained

To garnish:
8 black olives

1. Preheat broiler. Slice French bread in half horizontally. Cut each half in half crosswise. Place on a baking sheet.
2. Broil under preheated broiler until golden brown.
3. Spread toasted bread with tomato paste. Top with tomatoes, oregano or marjoram, salt, pepper and cheese.
4. Arrange anchovy fillets in a lattice pattern over cheese; garnish with olives.
5. Broil under preheated broiler about 10 minutes or until golden and bubbly.
6. Cut into thick slices. Serve hot. Makes 4 servings.

Variation
Substitute 2 cups chopped cooked ham and pimento-stuffed olives for anchovies and black olives. Sprinkle ham over tomato base; top with cheese. Garnish with a few sliced olives. Cook as above.

To prevent soggy sandwiches, spread soft butter, margarine, or soft cheese on the bread before adding the filling. Use toasted bread or crisp rolls for sandwiches that are made ahead. Add moist ingredients, such as tomato slices, immediately before serving. If the sandwich is for a packed lunch, wrap tomato slices separately.

To prevent sandwiches from drying out, wrap tightly with plastic wrap, or use plastic sandwich bags.

Many sandwiches can be frozen. However, hard-cooked eggs and mayonnaise do not freeze well. Hard-cooked egg whites become rubbery when frozen; mayonnaise separates.

Left to right: Broiled Asparagus & Cheese Sandwiches, French-Bread Pizzas

Broiled Asparagus & Cheese Sandwiches

4 whole-wheat-bread slices
3 tablespoons butter or margarine, room temperature
4 tomatoes, sliced
Salt
Freshly ground pepper
12 cooked asparagus spears
1 cup shredded Cheddar cheese (4 oz.)

1. Preheat broiler. Place bread slices on a baking sheet. Broil under preheated broiler until golden on 1 side.
2. Turn bread slices over; spread generously with butter or margarine.
3. Top with tomato slices. Sprinkle with salt and pepper. Arrange asparagus on tomatoes. Top with cheese.
4. Broil under preheated broiler 4 to 5 minutes or until cheese melts. Serve immediately. Makes 4 servings.

Indonesian Lamb Kabobs

1/2 cup plain yogurt
1 teaspoon ground ginger
1 garlic clove, crushed
1/4 teaspoon ground cumin
1/4 teaspoon ground coriander
2 tablespoons lemon juice
1 tablespoon vegetable oil
Salt
Freshly ground pepper
1 lb. lamb for stew, cut into 1-inch cubes
2 medium onions
1 green bell pepper, cut into 8 pieces
1 red bell pepper, cut into 8 pieces
12 medium button mushrooms

To serve:
Cooked saffron rice

1. In a medium, glass or stainless-steel bowl, combine yogurt, ginger, garlic, cumin, coriander, lemon juice, oil, salt and pepper. Stir in lamb until coated. Cover and refrigerate 2 to 3 hours or up to 24 hours.
2. Preheat broiler. Blanch onions in boiling water 3 minutes; drain. When cool, quarter onions.
3. Remove lamb from marinade with a slotted spoon; thread on 4 skewers, alternating with onion quarters, bell-pepper pieces and mushrooms. Place kabobs on a broiler-pan rack; brush with marinade.
4. Broil under preheated broiler 15 to 20 minutes or until lamb is cooked to desired doneness. Baste frequently with marinade during cooking. Serve with hot cooked rice. Makes 4 servings.

Beef, Apricot & Apple Kabobs

1 lb. beef round steak, thinly sliced
2 tablespoons butter or margarine
1 onion, chopped
2 cups fresh bread crumbs
1/2 teaspoon dried leaf thyme
2 tablespoons chopped fresh parsley
Salt
Freshly ground pepper
2 teaspoons lemon juice
1 egg, beaten
1 (1-lb.) can apricot halves, drained, or 12 fresh
    apricots, pitted, halved
3 green apples, cored, cut into 8 pieces
4 bay leaves
2 cups barbecue sauce

1. Cut beef into 12 strips about 1-1/2 inches wide.
2. Melt butter or margarine in a medium skillet. Add onion; sauté 5 minutes. Remove from heat; stir in bread crumbs, thyme, parsley, salt and pepper. Stir in lemon juice and egg. Divide mixture evenly among beef strips; roll up, enclosing stuffing.
3. Thread stuffed beef rolls on 4 skewers, alternating with apricots, apples and bay leaves. Brush with barbecue sauce. Place on a broiler-pan rack.
4. Broil under preheated broiler 20 to 25 minutes or until golden brown, turning frequently and basting with barbecue sauce.
5. Serve hot with any remaining barbecue sauce. Makes 4 servings.

Stroganoff-Topped Toast

1 lb. rare roast beef
Salt
Freshly ground black pepper
2 tablespoons butter or margarine
2 tablespoons finely chopped onion
6 oz. button mushrooms, sliced (about 2-1/2 cups)
5 tablespoons mayonnaise
5 tablespoons dairy sour cream
Pinch of red (cayenne) pepper
1 tablespoon chopped fresh chives

To serve:
Curly endive or watercress
8 whole-wheat-bread slices or rye-bread slices, toasted
Chopped chives

1. Slice beef across grain into fairly thick slices. Cut slices into small strips. Season with salt and black pepper.
2. Melt butter or margarine in a medium skillet. Add onion; sauté 2 minutes. Add mushrooms; cook 2 minutes. Remove from heat; stir in mayonnaise, sour cream, red pepper and 1 tablespoon chives.
3. Stir beef into stroganoff mixture; cook over low heat about 1 minute or until hot. Do not boil.
4. To serve, arrange endive or watercress on 4 individual plates; place 2 toast slices on each plate. Spoon stroganoff over toast. Garnish with chopped chives. Serve immediately. Makes 4 servings.

Clockwise from left: Indonesian Lamb Kabobs; Beef, Apricot & Apple Kabobs; Stroganoff-Topped Toast

Left to right: Crab Gratinée, Sole & Lime Pinwheels

Sole & Lime Pinwheels

6 tablespoons butter or margarine, room temperature
2 tablespoons chopped fresh chives
3/4 cup fresh bread crumbs
Grated peel of 1 lime
About 1/4 cup lime juice
Salt
Freshly ground pepper
8 skinless sole fillets

To garnish:
Lime twists
Fresh chives

1. Preheat broiler. Grease a shallow flameproof dish large enough to hold rolled fillets in 1 layer. In a small bowl, beat butter or margarine and chives until soft and creamy. Stir in bread crumbs, lime peel and enough lime juice to make a good spreading consistency for stuffing. Season with salt and pepper.
2. Spread sole fillets with equal amounts of stuffing. Roll up from wide end; secure rolls with wooden picks, using a small sharp-pointed knife to make an incision if necessary.
3. Place in greased dish; sprinkle with remaining lime juice.
4. Broil under preheated broiler 5 minutes. Turn over with tongs; broil 3 to 5 minutes or until fish tests done.
5. Garnish with lime twists and chives. Serve immediately. Makes 4 servings.

Crab Gratinée

8 oz. cooked crabmeat
4 oz. shrimp, cooked, peeled, deveined
3 tablespoons butter or margarine
2 tablespoons all-purpose flour
1/2 cup dry white wine
1 tablespoon lemon juice
2 teaspoons chopped fresh parsley
2 tablespoons whipping cream
1/2 head Chinese cabbage, shredded
6 tablespoons dry bread crumbs

To garnish:
Dill or parsley sprigs

1. Pick over crabmeat. In a medium bowl, combine crab-meat and shrimp. Set aside.
2. Melt 1 tablespoon butter or margarine in a medium saucepan. Stir in flour; cook 1 minute, stirring constantly. Gradually stir in wine and lemon juice to make a smooth sauce. Bring to a boil; cook 1 minute, stirring. Remove from heat; stir in parsley and cream.
3. Preheat broiler. Melt remaining 2 tablespoons butter or margarine in another medium saucepan. Add Chinese cabbage; cook over medium heat 1 to 2 minutes or until softened. Divide equally among 4 flameproof dishes or scallop shells. Make a hollow in center of each cabbage portion.
4. Fill each hollow with an equal amount of crab mixture. Spoon sauce over cabbage and crab mixture. Sprinkle with bread crumbs.
5. Broil under preheated broiler 4 to 5 minutes or until golden. Garnish with dill or parsley. Serve immediately. Makes 4 servings.

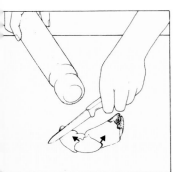

1/Using a knife and rolling pin, crack crab claws.

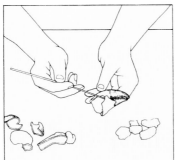

2/Remove crabmeat with a skewer or seafood fork.

Marinated Fish Kabobs

2 tablespoons honey
1 tablespoon vegetable oil
2 tablespoons soy sauce
1/2 cup white wine
1 teaspoon grated gingerroot
2 tablespoons chopped fresh chives
1-1/4 to 1-1/2 lb. cod or other firm-textured fish fillets, about 1 inch thick

1. In a glass or stainless-steel bowl, combine honey, oil, soy sauce, wine, gingerroot and chives. Set aside.
2. Cut fish fillets into 1-inch cubes. Add to marinade. Stir until coated. Cover and refrigerate 1 hour.
3. Preheat broiler. Grease a broiler-pan rack. Thread marinated fish on metal skewers. Place kabobs on greased rack.
4. Broil under preheated broiler about 8 minutes or until fish tests done, brushing with marinade.
5. Serve immediately. Makes 4 servings.

From the Pantry

Fish Paprika

6 tablespoons butter or margarine
2 large onions, sliced
3 canned pimentos, chopped
4 (4- to 6-oz.) pieces hake, haddock or whiting,
  thawed if frozen
Salt
Freshly ground pepper
8 oz. plain yogurt (1 cup)
2 teaspoons paprika

To garnish:
Plain croutons
Parsley sprigs

1. Preheat oven to 375F (190C). Grease a shallow baking dish large enough to hold fish in 1 layer. Melt 1/4 cup of butter or margarine in a medium skillet. Add onions; sauté about 5 minutes or until softened. Stir in pimentos.
2. Spoon 1/2 of onion mixture into greased dish. Top with fish; season fish with salt and pepper. Dot with remaining 2 tablespoons butter or margarine.
3. Bake in preheated oven, uncovered, 10 minutes. Top with remaining onion mixture. In a small bowl, combine yogurt and paprika; pour over fish. Bake 5 to 10 minutes or until fish tests done.
4. Garnish with croutons and parsley sprigs. Serve immediately. Makes 4 servings.

Herbed-Cheese Pasta

6 oz. green or white noodles
1 (3-oz.) pkg. cream cheese with herbs and garlic,
  room temperature
4 eggs, beaten
8 bacon slices, chopped
1 small onion, chopped
8 oz. mushrooms, sliced (about 3-1/4 cups)

To garnish:
1 tablespoon chopped fresh parsley
1 tomato, cut into wedges

1. Cook pasta in boiling salted water in a large saucepan according to package directions until tender. Do not overcook. Drain thoroughly; return to saucepan.
2. In a small bowl, beat cream cheese and eggs until combined; set aside.
3. In a medium skillet, cook bacon with no added fat until crisp and golden. Discard all but about 1 tablespoon fat. Stir in onion and mushrooms; cook 5 minutes.
4. Stir egg mixture and bacon mixture into cooked pasta. Stir over low heat until mixture thickens slightly.
5. Spoon into a warmed serving dish; sprinkle with parsley. Top with tomato wedges. Serve immediately. Makes 4 servings.

Tuna-Stuffed Tomatoes

4 large tomatoes
2 tablespoons butter or margarine
1 onion, chopped
1 (6-1/2-oz.) can tuna packed in oil, drained, flaked
1-1/2 cups fresh bread crumbs
1 tablespoon chopped fresh parsley
1 egg, beaten
Salt
Freshly ground pepper
1 (2-oz.) can anchovy fillets in oil

To garnish:
8 small black olives
Cilantro sprigs

1. Preheat oven to 350F (175C). Cut a thin slice from top of each tomato. Scoop out pulp; reserve pulp, discarding seeds.
2. Melt butter or margarine in a medium saucepan. Add onion; sauté 5 minutes. Remove from heat; stir in reserved tomato pulp, tuna, bread crumbs, parsley, egg, salt and pepper.
3. Spoon mixture into prepared tomatoes.
4. Drain anchovies, reserving oil; arrange anchovies over top of tomatoes. Place in an ovenproof dish; drizzle with anchovy oil.
5. Bake in preheated oven about 20 minutes or until heated through. Garnish with black olives and cilantro. Serve hot with crusty bread. Makes 4 servings.

Top to bottom: Tuna-Stuffed Tomatoes, Fish Paprika

Spicy Beef Stir-Fry

10 oz. roast beef, cut into thin strips
6 tablespoons orange juice
1 tablespoon lemon juice
2 tablespoons black-bean sauce or 2 tablespoons
    concentrated beef stock
2 tablespoons chili powder
1 teaspoon cornstarch
Salt
Freshly ground black pepper
3 tablespoons vegetable oil
1 large red bell pepper, sliced
1 onion, sliced
1 (10-oz.) pkg. frozen green peas

1. In a medium glass or stainless-steel bowl, combine beef, orange juice, lemon juice, black-bean sauce or beef stock, chili powder, cornstarch, salt and black pepper. Cover and marinate 1 hour.
2. Heat oil in a large skillet or wok; add bell pepper and onion. Stir-fry over high heat 2 to 3 minutes.
3. Add marinated beef and marinade mixture; stir-fry 2 minutes. Add peas; stir-fry 1 minute.
4. Serve hot with Chinese noodles. Makes 4 servings.

Beef Patties with Chasseur Sauce

Chasseur Sauce:
2 tablespoons vegetable oil
1 bacon slice, chopped
1 small celery stalk, chopped
1 small carrot, chopped
2 tablespoons all-purpose flour
1/2 cup beef stock
1/2 cup dry white wine
1 teaspoon tomato paste
1 teaspoon Dijon-style mustard
2 large tomatoes, peeled, seeded, chopped
Salt
Freshly ground pepper
2 tablespoons butter or margarine
4 oz. button mushrooms, chopped
1 small onion, chopped
2 tablespoons sherry or brandy, if desired
4 (4- to 6-oz.) beef patties

To serve:
4 thick bread slices, toasted
1 tablespoon chopped fresh parsley

1. To make sauce, heat oil in a medium saucepan. Add bacon, celery and carrot; sauté about 5 minutes or until vegetables are softened.

Left to right: Beef Patties with Chasseur Sauce, Crispy Beef & Bean Bundles

2. Stir in flour. Cook, stirring constantly, over low heat about 15 minutes or until flour is a rich brown color. Gradually stir in stock and wine. Stir in tomato paste, mustard and tomatoes. Cook over a medium heat 5 minutes.
3. Press sauce through a fine sieve. Reheat; season with salt and pepper.
4. Preheat broiler. Melt butter or margarine in a medium saucepan. Add mushrooms and onion; cook about 5 minutes or until softened. Stir into sauce with sherry or brandy, if desired. Keep warm.
5. Place beef patties on a broiler-pan rack. Broil under preheated broiler 5 to 8 minutes on each side, depending on size and desired degree of doneness.
6. To serve, place a bread slice on each of 4 individual plates. Top each bread slice with a broiled patty; spoon sauce over patties. Sprinkle with parsley; serve with broiled tomatoes. Makes 4 servings.

Crispy Beef & Bean Bundles

8 oz. lean ground beef
2 oz. mushrooms, sliced
1 (15-oz.) can refried beans
1 teaspoon chili powder
Salt
Freshly ground pepper
8 (6- to 8-inch) flour tortillas
2 tablespoons butter or margarine
1 tablespoon vegetable oil

To garnish:
Red- and green-bell-pepper rings

---

1. In a large skillet, cook beef with no added fat over medium heat. Stirring to break up beef, cook about 5 minutes or until lightly browned.
2. Stir in mushrooms; cook 5 minutes. Remove from heat; drain off excess fat. Stir in beans, chili powder, salt and pepper.

3. Spoon beef-and-bean mixture equally into center of each tortilla. Fold opposite sides of each tortilla over filling slightly overlapping at center. Fold remaining 2 sides in to enclose filling completely. Press down gently to seal.
4. Heat butter and oil in a large skillet. Add filled tortillas; cook over medium heat until crisp and golden on both sides. Drain on paper towels.
5. Arrange on a platter; garnish with bell-pepper rings. Makes 4 servings.

1/Fold opposite sides of each tortilla over filling, slightly overlapping at center.

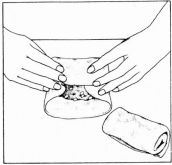

2/Fold remaining 2 sides in to enclose filling completely.

Baked Eggs Mornay

4-1/2 cups chopped, peeled potatoes (about 1-1/2 lb.)
2 tablespoons butter or margarine
Salt
White pepper
4 hard-cooked eggs, halved

Sauce:
3 tablespoons butter or margarine
3 tablespoons all-purpose flour
1 cup milk
1/2 teaspoon prepared mustard
3/4 cup shredded Cheddar cheese (3 oz.)
1 tablespoon chopped fresh chives
Salt
White pepper

To garnish:
Parsley sprigs

---

1. Grease 4 (2-cup) flameproof dishes or a shallow 2-quart flameproof dish. In a large saucepan, cook potatoes in boiling salted water about 20 minutes or until tender. Drain and mash potatoes. Stir in butter or margarine, salt and white pepper.
2. Spoon mashed potatoes into a pastry bag fitted with a large star-shaped tip. Pipe potatoes around edges of individual greased dishes or large greased dish.
3. Preheat broiler. Divide hard-cooked eggs among individual dishes or place in large dish.
4. To make sauce, melt butter or margarine in a medium saucepan. Stir in flour; cook 1 minute, stirring. Gradually stir in milk. Bring to a boil; cook 2 to 3 minutes, stirring. Stir in mustard, cheese, chives, salt and white pepper. Spoon sauce over eggs.
5. Broil under preheated broiler 5 to 10 minutes or until golden and bubbly. Serve immediately. Makes 4 servings.

Dilled Crabmeat Soufflé

3 tablespoons butter or margarine
3 tablespoons all-purpose flour
1 cup milk
1/4 cup whipping cream
Salt
White pepper
1/2 teaspoon dry mustard
4 eggs, separated
2 (6-1/2-oz.) cans crabmeat, drained
2 tablespoons chopped fresh dill or 2 teaspoons
  dried dill weed

---

1. Preheat oven to 375F (190C). Grease a 7-inch soufflé dish. Melt butter or margarine in a medium saucepan. Stir in flour; cook 1 minute, stirring. Gradually stir in milk; cook, stirring constantly, until sauce is thickened and comes to a boil. Stir in cream, salt, white pepper and mustard. Remove from heat.
2. Beat in egg yolks, 1 at a time, beating throughly after each addition. Pick over crabmeat. Fold in crabmeat and dill.
3. In a medium bowl, beat egg whites until stiff but not dry. Fold beaten egg whites into crabmeat mixture. Pour into greased soufflé dish.
4. Bake in preheated oven 40 to 45 minutes or until puffed and golden brown. Serve immediately with a tossed salad. Makes 3 to 4 servings.

Dutch-Cheese Fondue

1 cup dry white wine or apple cider
1 garlic clove, crushed
1/2 teaspoon freshly grated nutmeg
4 cups shredded Gouda cheese or Edam cheese (1 lb.)
1 tablespoon cornstarch
Salt
White pepper
2 to 3 tablespoons kirsch
1 large French-bread loaf, cubed

---

1. Heat wine or cider, garlic and nutmeg in a fondue pot or heavy saucepan until hot but not boiling.
2. In a medium bowl, combine cheese and cornstarch. Stir into wine mixture, a little at a time. Stir over very low heat until thick and creamy.
3. Season with salt and white pepper; stir in kirsch to taste.
4. Serve hot fondue with French bread. Makes 4 servings.

Deviled Spanish Pizza

Sauce:
1 (1-lb.) can tomatoes, drained, chopped
1 small onion, chopped
2 tablespoons tomato paste
2 teaspoons dried leaf oregano
Salt
Freshly ground pepper

Dough:
1-1/2 cups self-rising flour
Freshly ground pepper
1/4 cup milk
1/4 cup olive oil

Topping:
6 oz. mozzarella cheese, sliced
4 oz. salami, sliced
1 tablespoon grated Parmesan cheese
4 to 6 pimento-stuffed olives, sliced

1. Preheat oven to 400F (205C). Grease a baking sheet. To make sauce, place tomatoes, onion, tomato paste and oregano in a medium saucepan. Cook over medium heat 15 to 20 minutes or until thick, stirring occasionally.
2. To make dough, in a medium bowl, combine flour and pepper. Stir in milk and olive oil to form a soft dough.
3. On a lightly floured surface, knead dough until smooth. Roll out dough to a 10-inch circle. Place on greased baking sheet. Spoon sauce over dough circle to within 1 inch of edge.
4. Top with mozzarella cheese, salami, Parmesan cheese and olives.
5. Bake in preheated oven 30 minutes or until crust is golden brown.
6. Cut into wedges. Serve hot with a tossed green salad. Makes 2 servings.

Top to bottom: Deviled Spanish Pizza, Dutch-Cheese Fondue

Spanish-Style Omelet

2 tablespoons butter or margarine
1 large onion, sliced
4 bacon slices, chopped
2 cups diced cooked potatoes (about 12 oz.)
1 red bell pepper, chopped
1 green bell pepper, chopped
4 eggs, beaten
Salt
Freshly ground pepper
1 teaspoon dried leaf marjoram
1/2 cup shredded Cheddar cheese (2 oz.)
6 pimento-stuffed olives, sliced
1 teaspoon paprika

1. Preheat broiler. Melt butter or margarine in a large heavy skillet. Add onion and bacon; sauté until bacon is crisp and lightly browned.
2. Add potatoes and bell peppers; cook 2 minutes. In a medium bowl, beat eggs with salt, pepper and marjoram. Pour over potato mixture; cook over low heat until mixture is almost set. Sprinkle with cheese, olives and paprika.
3. Broil under preheated broiler about 3 minutes or until cheese melts.
4. Serve hot with warm crusty bread and a vegetable salad. Makes 4 servings.

Pickled-Herring Salad

1 (12-oz.) jar pickled herrings, drained
3 dill pickles, thinly sliced
2 red-skinned apples, cored, sliced into rings
1 bunch green onions, chopped
1/2 cup dairy sour cream
1/2 teaspoon dried dill weed

1. Cut herrings into thin strips; place in a medium bowl.
2. Add dill pickles, apples, green onions, sour cream and dill; stir until combined.
3. Spoon into a chilled serving dish; serve with warm crusty bread. Makes 4 servings.

Camembert Puffs

8 individual wedges Camembert cheese, well-chilled
2 tablespoons all-purpose flour
2 eggs, beaten
1-1/2 cups fresh white-bread crumbs
Vegetable oil for deep-frying

To serve:
1/2 cup gooseberry, damson or cherry conserve, chilled

1. Dust cheese wedges with flour. Dip floured wedges into beaten egg; coat with bread crumbs. Set aside.
2. Heat oil in a deep saucepan to 375F (190C) or until a 1-inch bread cube turns golden brown in 40 seconds. Add coated cheese wedges to hot oil. Deep-fry 3 to 4 minutes or until crisp and golden.
3. Drain on paper towels. Serve immediately with fruit conserve. Makes 4 servings.

Cheese & Walnut Croquettes with Watercress Dip

1 cup finely chopped walnuts
1-1/2 cups fresh bread crumbs
1/2 small onion, grated
1/2 cup shredded Edam cheese (2 oz.)
1 tablespoon chopped fresh parsley
Salt
Freshly ground pepper
1 egg, beaten
1 to 2 tablespoons milk
2 tablespoons vegetable oil

Watercress Dip:
1 bunch watercress, finely chopped
1/2 cup dairy sour cream
1 teaspoon Italian seasoning
Pinch of freshly grated nutmeg
Salt
White pepper

1. In a medium bowl, combine walnuts, bread crumbs, onion, cheese, parsley, salt and pepper. Stir in egg and 1 tablespoon milk. Stir in additional milk, if necessary. Shape mixture into 12 equal croquettes.
2. Heat oil in a large skillet. Add croquettes; sauté over medium heat about 10 minutes or until browned on all sides. Drain on paper towels.
3. To make dip, blend watercress, sour cream, Italian seasoning, nutmeg, salt and white pepper. Spoon into a small serving bowl.
4. Serve warm croquettes with dip. Makes 4 servings.

Clockwise from left: Spanish-Style Omelet, Pickled-Herring Salad, Camembert Puffs with fruit conserve

Cottage-Cheese Pancakes

Spreads:
2 (3-oz.) pkgs. cream cheese, room temperature
6 tablespoons dairy sour cream
1 (2-oz.) jar red lumpfish caviar
Fresh chopped chives
1 (3-3/4-oz.) can sardines packed in oil, drained
1 tablespoon lemon juice
Paprika

Pancakes:
1/4 cup all-purpose flour
1/4 teaspoon salt
2 tablespoons butter or margarine, melted
3/4 cup cream-style cottage cheese
3 eggs, separated
Butter or margarine for cooking

Serve these small, savory pancakes as an appetizer.

1. To make spreads, in a blender or food processor fitted with a steel blade, process 1 package cream cheese, 3 tablespoons sour cream and caviar until smooth. Spoon into a small serving dish; sprinkle with chopped chives.
2. In a blender or food processor fitted with a steel blade, process remaining package of cream cheese, remaining 3 tablespoons sour cream, sardines and lemon juice until smooth. Spoon into a small serving dish; sprinkle with paprika.
3. To make pancakes, in a medium bowl, combine flour and salt. In a small bowl, combine butter or margarine, cottage cheese and egg yolks. Stir cottage-cheese mixture into flour mixture until blended.
4. In a medium bowl, beat egg whites until stiff but not dry; fold beaten egg whites into batter.
5. Heat 1 to 2 tablespoons butter or margarine in a large skillet. Drop batter by rounded tablespoonfuls into skillet, spacing pancakes well apart. Cook over medium heat 2 to 3 minutes. Turn pancakes over with a wide spatula; cook 2 to 3 minutes or until golden brown. Remove from skillet; keep warm. Repeat with additional butter or margarine and remaining batter.
6. Serve spreads with warm pancakes. Makes 12 to 14 small pancakes.

Tropical Kabobs

5 all-beef frankfurters
1 (15-oz.) can pineapple chunks in natural juice
2 green bell peppers, cut into 1-inch pieces
1 tablespoon soy sauce
1 teaspoon vegetable oil
1 teaspoon grated gingerroot
Salt
Freshly ground pepper
2 teaspoons cornstarch
Water

1. Preheat broiler. Score frankfurters diagonally along 1 side; cut each scored frankfurter into 4 pieces.
2. Drain pineapple chunks, reserving juice.
3. Thread frankfurters on 4 skewers, alternating with pineapple chunks and bell-pepper pieces. Place kabobs on a broiler-pan rack.
4. In a small saucepan, combine reserved pineapple juice, soy sauce, oil, gingerroot, salt and pepper. Brush kabobs with a little of pineapple mixture.
5. Broil under preheated broiler until hot and bubbly, basting occasionally with sauce.
6. In a small bowl, combine cornstarch and a little water; stir mixture into remaining sauce. Boil, stirring constantly, until thickened.
7. Serve hot kabobs with sauce. Serve with hot cooked rice or cooked noodles. Makes 4 servings.

Left to right: Tropical Kabobs, Cottage-Cheese Pancakes with Spreads, Stuffed Onions

Stuffed Onions

4 large Spanish onions, peeled
Salt
8 oz. lean ground beef
2 garlic cloves, crushed
1/2 cup pine nuts
1 teaspoon Italian seasoning
Freshly ground pepper
1 cup fresh bread crumbs
3/4 cup shredded Cheddar cheese (3 oz.)
1 egg, beaten
1/2 cup plain yogurt

1. Boil onions in a large saucepan of salted boiling water 10 minutes. Drain, reserving about 1/2 cup of cooking liquid.
2. Scoop out centers of onions with a small knife or spoon; reserve for another dish. Set hollowed-out onions aside.
3. Preheat oven to 375F (190C). In a medium skillet, cook beef with no added fat over medium heat. Cook, stirring constantly, until lightly browned. Add garlic, pine nuts, Italian seasoning, salt and pepper. Cook 5 minutes. Remove from heat; stir in bread crumbs, cheese and egg until blended.
4. Fill onions with beef mixture; place filled onions in an ovenproof dish large enough to hold them in 1 layer. Pour reserved cooking liquid around stuffed onions. Cover with a lid or foil.
5. Bake in preheated oven 30 minutes. Uncover; bake 30 minutes or until tender.
6. Serve hot with yogurt. Makes 4 servings.

Clockwise from left: Fish & Egg Puff, Potato & Fish Bake, Seafood Crepes

Potato & Fish Bake

3 cups chopped peeled potatoes (about 1 lb.)
Salt
2 tablespoons butter or margarine
White pepper
1 cup shredded Cheddar cheese (4 oz.)
4 (4-oz.) pieces cod or other fish
1 cup wine
1 shallot, chopped
1 bay leaf
2 tablespoons all-purpose flour
2 tablespoons butter or margarine, room temperature

To garnish:
Lemon wedges
Parsley sprigs

1. Grease 4 large scallop shells or 4 individual baking dishes. Cook potatoes in a large saucepan of boiling salted water about 20 minutes or until tender. Drain and mash potatoes. Stir in butter or margarine, salt and white pepper. Stir in 1/2 of cheese. Spoon into a pastry bag fitted with a large star-shaped tip. Pipe swirls of potato mixture around edges of greased scallop shells or individual dishes. Set aside.

2. Preheat oven to 350F (175C). Arrange fish in a baking dish. Add wine, shallot, bay leaf and enough water to cover fish. Cover with a lid or foil.

3. Bake fish in preheated oven 8 to 10 minutes or until fish tests done. Remove fish from cooking liquid, reserving liquid. Let fish cool slightly. Flake fish; set aside.

4. Preheat broiler. Strain reserved cooking liquid into a medium saucepan; boil until reduced to 1 cup. In a small bowl, blend flour and butter or margarine into a paste. Whisk paste into hot liquid. Cook until thickened. Stir flaked fish into sauce. Season with salt and white pepper. Spoon sauce mixture into center of piped potatoes in scallop shells or dishes; sprinkle with remaining cheese.

5. Broil under preheated broiler 5 minutes or until potatoes are golden and sauce is bubbly.

6. Garnish with lemon wedges and parsley sprigs. Makes 4 servings.

Seafood Crepes

Crepe Batter:
1-1/4 cups all-purpose flour
3 eggs
1-1/2 cups milk
1/3 cup butter or margarine, melted
Butter or margarine for cooking

Filling:
1/4 cup butter or margarine
1/4 cup all-purpose flour
1/2 cup dry white wine
1-1/2 cups fish or chicken stock
1 tablespoon tomato paste
Salt
Freshly ground pepper
1/4 cup whipping cream
1 tablespoon chopped fresh parsley
1 (4-1/4-oz.) can shrimp, drained
1 (8-3/4-oz.) jar mussels, drained, chopped
1 (6-1/2-oz.) can crabmeat, drained, flaked
1 teaspoon lemon juice

Using a blender to make the crepe batter saves time.

1. Place flour, eggs and milk in a blender or food processor fitted with a steel blade; process until smooth, scraping down bowl sides as necessary. Pour melted butter slowly into batter with machine motor running; process until combined. Pour batter into a large measuring cup or small pitcher. Cover and refrigerate 1 hour.
2. To cook crepes, melt 1 tablespoon butter or margarine in a 6- or 7-inch skillet or crepe pan. Pour in just enough batter to cover bottom of pan in a thin layer. Cook over medium heat 1-1/2 minutes or until small bubbles begin to form on surface of crepe. Turn crepe; cook 1-1/2 minutes. Remove to a flat plate; repeat process with remaining batter. Add additional butter or margarine to skillet as necessary.
3. To make filling, melt butter or margarine in a medium saucepan. Stir in flour; cook 1 minute, stirring. Gradually stir in wine and stock. Bring to a boil; cook 2 to 3 minutes, stirring. Stir in tomato paste, salt and pepper. Cook over low heat 10 minutes. Stir in cream and 1/2 of parsley.
4. Preheat oven to 350F (175C). Grease a 13" x 9" baking pan. In a medium bowl, combine shrimp, mussels and crabmeat; stir in 1/2 of sauce. Fill 15 crepes with an equal amount of filling; roll up. Place filled crepes, seam-side down, in greased pan.
5. Stir lemon juice into remaining sauce; pour over crepes.
6. Bake in preheated oven 10 to 15 minutes or until heated through.
7. Sprinkle with remaining parsley; serve hot. Makes 5 servings of 3 crepes each.

Fish & Egg Puffs

1/2 (17-1/4-oz.) pkg. frozen puff pastry
  (1 sheet), thawed
4 small flounder, sole, haddock or halibut fillets
2 hard-cooked eggs, sliced
1/2 cup condensed cream of mushroom soup, undiluted
1 teaspoon lemon juice
4 teaspoons capers, drained, chopped
1 tablespoon chopped chives
Salt
Freshly ground pepper
1 egg yolk beaten with 1 tablespoon water for glaze

---

1. Preheat oven to 425F (220C). Unfold pastry; lay flat on a lightly floured surface. Roll out pastry with a lightly floured rolling pin to a 13-inch square. Cut off 2 (1-inch) strips down length and width of pastry to make a 12-inch square. Reserve pastry strips for decorations. Cut pastry into 4 (6-inch) squares; place on ungreased baking sheet.
2. Place 1 fish fillet in center of each pastry square. Top with 2 or 3 egg slices. In a small bowl, combine soup, lemon juice, capers, chives, salt and pepper; spoon soup mixture over eggs.
3. Brush pastry edges with egg glaze. Bring opposite corners of pastry together in center to enclose filling. Pinch pastry edges to seal. Poke small hole in center of each puff to allow steam to escape. Cut reserved pastry strips into decorative shapes. Brush decorations with egg glaze; attach to puffs. Brush puffs all over with egg glaze.
4. Bake in preheated oven 20 to 25 minutes or until puffed and golden brown. Serve hot with tossed green salad or sliced tomatoes. Makes 4 servings.

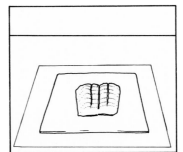
1/Place 1 fish fillet in center of each pastry square.

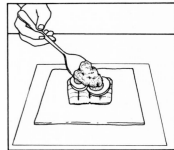
2/Spoon soup mixture over eggs.

3/Bring opposite corners of pastry together in center to enclose filling.

4/Attach decorations to puffs.

Salads, Pastries & Pâtés

Italian Platter

Dressing:
3 tablespoons red-wine vinegar
1 tablespoon lemon juice
1 small garlic clove, crushed
1-1/2 teaspoons prepared coarse mustard
1/2 cup olive oil or other vegetable oil
Salt
Freshly ground pepper

Platter:
4 medium new potatoes, boiled in skins
1/4 cup mayonnaise
1 tablespoon chopped fresh parsley
1 (14-oz.) can artichoke hearts, drained
1 (14-oz.) can cannellini beans or
   white kidney beans, drained
1 (4-1/2-oz.) can sardines in oil, drained
10 salami slices, rolled into cornets
2 hard-cooked eggs, quartered
2 medium tomatoes
1 (2-oz.) can anchovy fillets in oil, drained

---

1. To make dressing, in a small bowl, combine vinegar, lemon juice, garlic and mustard. Gradually whisk in oil until thickened. Season with salt and pepper.
2. To make potato salad, cut potatoes into thick slices; place in a medium bowl. Stir in mayonnaise, parsley, salt and pepper.
3. Arrange artichoke hearts, beans, sardines, salami, hard-cooked eggs and potato salad around edge of a large platter like spokes of a wheel.
4. Slice tomatoes; place tomatoes in center of platter. Cover with an anchovy lattice.
5. Drizzle dressing over whole platter; serve with crusty bread. Makes 4 servings.

Ham-Stuffed Papaya

4 large papayas, about 8 oz. each
2 teaspoons fresh lime juice
12 oz. cooked ham, cut into 1/2-inch cubes
1 red bell pepper, chopped
1/2 cup mayonnaise
2 teaspoons prepared horseradish
Finely grated peel of 1 lime
Buttered bread triangles

To garnish:
Lime twists

Sometimes called pawpaws, papayas, with pink-orange flesh, are somewhat similar to melons. Serve half a papaya per person for an unusual starter.

1. Slice papayas in half lengthwise; scoop out and discard seeds. Carefully scoop out flesh with a melon baller, or cut into small cubes, leaving shells intact.
2. In a medium bowl, combine papaya balls or cubes, lime juice, ham, bell pepper, mayonnaise, horseradish and lime peel.
3. Spoon papaya-and-shrimp mixture into reserved shells. Place 2 filled shells on each of 4 individual serving plates.
4. Refrigerate 30 minutes or until slightly chilled before serving. Serve with buttered bread. Garnish with lime twists. Makes 4 servings.

A papaya resembles an elongated melon. A papaya is ripe when the skin turns yellow and feels tender when lightly pressed at the stalk end.

To prepare a papaya, halve lengthwise; scoop out seeds with a metal spoon. The seeds have a very peppery taste and are usually discarded. After removing the seeds, scoop the flesh from the shell. Or, the papaya can be peeled and sliced.

Top to bottom: Ham-Stuffed Papaya, Italian Platter

Cucumber, Melon & Ham Salad

1 small honeydew or other melon
8 oz. cooked ham
4 tomatoes, quartered
1 cup black grapes, halved, seeded
1/4 cucumber, thinly sliced

Dressing:
1/4 cup dairy sour cream
2 tablespoons chopped green onion
1 teaspoon chopped fresh mint
Salt
White pepper

To garnish:
Fresh mint sprigs

1. Slice melon in half; scoop out and discard seeds. Remove flesh with a melon baller, or cut into 1-inch cubes. Reserve melon shells for serving, if desired.
2. Cut ham into thin julienne strips. In a medium bowl, combine ham strips, melon ball or cubes, tomatoes, grapes and cucumber.
3. To make dressing, in a small bowl, combine sour cream, green onion, mint, salt and white pepper. Dressing can be made 24 hours ahead, if desired. Cover and refrigerate if not using immediately.
4. To serve, pour dressing over salad; toss until coated with dressing. Spoon into a serving bowl or melon shells.
5. Garnish with mint sprigs. Makes 4 servings.

Left to right: Cucumber, Melon & Ham Salad; Midsummer Chicken; Smoked-Trout & Orange Salad

Smoked-Trout & Orange Salad

12 oz. smoked-trout fillets, skinned
1/2 cucumber, thinly sliced
3 oranges, sectioned
3 celery stalks, thinly sliced

Dressing:
1/2 medium apple, grated
1 tablespoon lemon juice
3 tablespoons mayonnaise
1-1/2 teaspoons prepared horseradish

To serve:
Few lettuce leaves
Red (cayenne) pepper

1. Flake trout into small pieces. In a medium bowl, combine flaked trout, cucumber, orange sections and celery.
2. To make dressing, in a small bowl, combine apple, lemon juice, mayonnaise and horseradish.
3. To serve, line individual serving dishes with lettuce leaves. Top with salad. Spoon dressing over salad.
4. Cover and refrigerate until chilled. Garnish with red pepper. Makes 4 servings.

Midsummer Chicken

1 lb. cooked chicken, skinned, boned
1/2 cup dry white wine
1 teaspoon lemon juice
2 teaspoons grated onion
1 teaspoon chopped fresh tarragon
Pinch of onion salt
4 oranges, sectioned
1/4 head endive or leaf lettuce, torn into bite-sized
  pieces
1 bunch watercress, large stems removed
1/2 cup toasted pine nuts or walnuts

Dressing:
1 (3-oz.) pkg. cream cheese, room temperature
1/2 pint dairy sour cream (1 cup)
3 drops hot-pepper sauce
Salt
Freshly ground pepper

To garnish:
Blanched orange peel, cut into julienne strips

1. Slice chicken into thin strips. In a medium bowl, combine chicken strips, wine, lemon juice, onion, tarragon, onion salt and orange sections. Cover and let stand 20 minutes to blend flavors.
2. Meanwhile, toss lettuce or endive with watercress; line a serving plate with watercress mixture.
3. Drain marinade from chicken mixture, reserving marinade. Stir pine nuts or walnuts into chicken mixture. Spoon chicken mixture over watercress mixture on plates.
4. To make dressing, in a small bowl, combine cheese, sour cream, hot-pepper sauce, salt and pepper. Add about 2 tablespoons marinade or enough to give dressing a thick pouring consistency. Pour dressing over chicken mixture.
5. Garnish with orange peel. Makes 4 servings.

Tropical Curried-Chicken Salad

12 oz. cooked chicken, skinned, boned
2 ripe bananas, sliced
1 tablespoon lemon juice
1/2 cup cashew nuts
1/4 cup raisins
1/4 cup chopped dried apricots

Dressing:
3 tablespoons mayonnaise
1 tablespoon finely chopped onion
1/2 teaspoon hot Madras curry powder
1/2 teaspoon lemon juice
2 tablespoons grated apple
1 teaspoon mango chutney
Pinch of salt

To garnish:
2 tablespoons shredded coconut, toasted

For special occasions, serve this salad on plain or spiced poppadums. Poppadums, a thin bread from India, are available in specialty stores. If poppadums are not available, use corn tortillas that have been shaped into bowls and fried.

1. Cut chicken into small pieces. In a serving bowl, combine chicken pieces, bananas and lemon juice. Stir in cashews, raisins and dried apricots.
2. To make dressing, in a small bowl, combine mayonnaise, onion, curry powder, lemon juice, apple, chutney and salt.
3. Spoon dressing over salad; toss to coat with dressing.
4. Cover and refrigerate until chilled. Garnish with toasted coconut. Makes 4 servings.

Spicy Mexican Salad

1 (12-oz.) can whole-kernel corn, drained
1 (15-oz.) can red kidney beans, drained
1 small onion, thinly sliced into rings
1 small green bell pepper, thinly sliced
6 oz. cooked chorizo sausage, skinned, sliced,
    or salami, chopped

Dressing:
1/4 cup mayonnaise
2 tablespoons chili salsa
1/2 teaspoon mild chili powder
1 tablespoon finely chopped red bell pepper
Pinch of salt

Use this spicy dressing in salads and sandwiches, or as a delicious topping for baked potatoes.

1. In a large salad bowl, combine corn, kidney beans, onion, green bell pepper and chorizo or salami.
2. To make dressing, in a small bowl, combine mayonnaise, chili salsa, chili powder, red bell pepper and salt.
3. Spoon dressing over salad; toss to coat with dressing.
4. Cover and refrigerate until chilled. Serve with tortillas, corn chips or crisp crackers. Makes 4 servings.

Seafood Pasta

6 oz. pasta twists (about 1-1/2 cups)
1 ripe avocado, sliced
2 teaspoons lemon juice
6 oz. shrimp, cooked, peeled, deveined
1 (8-3/4-oz.) jar mussels, drained
3 tomatoes, cut into wedges
4 or 5 mushrooms, sliced

Dressing:
2 tablespoons mayonnaise
2 tablespoons dairy sour cream
1 garlic clove, crushed
2 teaspoons chopped chives
Salt
Freshly ground pepper

To garnish:
3 or 4 whole unpeeled cooked shrimp

---

1. Cook pasta twists in a large saucepan of boiling salted water according to package directions until tender. Do not overcook. Drain and cool.
2. In a medium bowl, toss avocado slices in lemon juice. Stir in cooled pasta, shrimp, mussels, tomatoes and mushrooms until combined.
3. To make dressing, in a small bowl, combine mayonnaise, sour cream, garlic, chives, salt and pepper.
4. Fold dressing into salad; spoon into a serving dish. Cover and refrigerate until chilled. Garnish with whole shrimp. Makes 4 servings.

Top to bottom: Seafood Pasta, Tropical Curried-Chicken Salad served in a poppadum

Chicken & Ham Loaf

1 unsliced sandwich-bread loaf
6 tablespoons butter or margarine
2 small onions, finely chopped
8 oz. mushrooms, thinly sliced (about 3-1/4 cups)
1 tablespoon chopped fresh parsley
Salt
Freshly ground pepper
6 bacon slices, crisp-cooked, crumbled
2 cups chopped cooked ham (about 8 oz.)
1/4 teaspoon rubbed sage
1/4 teaspoon dried leaf thyme
2 tablespoons dry sherry, if desired
2 cups chopped cooked chicken

To garnish:
Cilantro

---

1. Preheat oven to 375F (190C). Cut a 1/2-inch slice length-wise off top of loaf. Carefully pull out soft bread inside, leaving a 1/2-inch-thick wall. Make bread crumbs from soft bread.
2. Melt 1/4 cup butter or margarine; brush loaf, inside and out, with melted butter or margarine. Replace lid; brush lid with remaining butter or margarine. Place on a baking sheet.
3. Bake in preheated oven 10 minutes or until crisp and golden.
4. Melt remaining 2 tablespoons butter or margarine in a medium skillet. Add onions; sauté 5 minutes or until soft. Add mushrooms; cook 2 minutes. Stir in parsley, salt and pepper. Remove from heat.
5. In a medium bowl, combine bacon, ham and 3 tablespoons bread crumbs. Stir in sage, thyme and sherry, if desired.
6. Press 1/2 of ham mixture into bread case. Cover with 1/2 of mushroom mixture. Cover with chicken; cover chicken with remaining mushroom mixture. Press remaining ham mixture over mushroom mixture. Replace lid; wrap loaf in foil.
7. Bake in preheated oven 50 minutes or until center is hot. Serve loaf hot or cold. Cut into thick slices to serve. Garnish with parsley. Makes 6 to 8 servings.

Pear Waldorf Salad

8 oz. cooked chicken, skinned, boned
1 head lettuce, shredded
2 celery stalks, chopped
1 red bell pepper, sliced
1/4 cup walnut halves
1 cup seedless green grapes, halved
1 pear, peeled, cored, sliced

Dressing:
2 tablespoons plain yogurt
2 tablespoons mayonnaise
2 tablespoons grated cucumber
1 teaspoon grated onion
1/2 teaspoon chopped fresh tarragon
Salt
Freshly ground pepper

To garnish:
1 pear, cored, sliced
Fresh tarragon sprigs

This is a variation of classic Waldorf Salad, so called because it was invented by the chef of the Waldorf Hotel in New York. Pear Waldorf Salad combines pears with classic ingredients and a tasty cucumber-and-tarragon dressing.

1. Cut chicken into small pieces. In a large salad bowl, combine lettuce, celery, bell pepper, walnuts, grapes, pear and chicken pieces.
2. To make dressing, in a small bowl, combine yogurt, mayonnaise, cucumber, onion and tarragon. Season with salt and pepper.
3. Spoon dressing over salad ingredients; toss to coat with dressing.
4. Garnish with pear slices and a few tarragon sprigs. Makes 4 servings.

Variation
Pear Waldorf Salad with Sour-Cream Dressing: To make dressing, in a small bowl, combine 2 tablespoons dairy sour cream, 2 tablespoons mayonnaise, 1 tablespoon grated zucchini or cucumber, 2 teaspoons grated onion, 1 tablespoon chopped peanuts, salt and freshly ground pepper.

Left to right: Chicken & Ham Loaf, Pear Waldorf Salad

Smoked-Salmon Mousse

1 lb. smoked-salmon trimmings
2 tablespoons lemon juice
1/2 cup mayonnaise
1 medium onion, grated
2 tablespoons chopped chives
1 (1/4-oz.) envelope unflavored gelatin (1 tablespoon)
1/4 cup chicken broth or water
3/4 cup whipping cream
Salt
White pepper
Hot-pepper sauce
2 egg whites
To garnish:
Cucumber slices
Pimento-stuffed olives

1. In a blender or food processor fitted with a steel blade, process salmon pieces until almost smooth. Spoon into a medium bowl; stir in lemon juice, mayonnaise, onion and chives until thoroughly blended.
2. In a small saucepan, combine gelatin and broth or water. Stir well; let stand 3 minutes. Stir over low heat until gelatin dissolves; set aside to cool. Stir gelatin into salmon mixture.
3. In a medium bowl, whip cream until stiff peaks form. Fold into salmon mixture. Season with salt, white pepper and hot-pepper sauce. Refrigerate until mixture mounds when dropped from a spoon.
4. Beat egg whites in a medium bowl until stiff peaks form. Fold beaten egg whites into salmon mixture. Rinse a 4- to 5-cup decorative mold with cold water. Spoon mixture into mold; smooth top. Refrigerate 3 hours or until set.
5. To serve, run a knife tip around top of mold to loosen. Invert mold on a serving plate. Wet a clean dish towel with hot water; wring dry. Wrap hot towel around outside of mold a few seconds. Remove towel and mold. Garnish mousse with cucumber slices and pimento-stuffed olives. Serve with assorted crackers or cocktail breads. Makes 6 to 8 servings.

Creamy Chicken Loaf en Croûte

Pastry:
1-1/2 cups all-purpose flour
1 teaspoon grated lemon peel
1/2 teaspoon salt
1/2 cup butter or margarine
3 to 4 tablespoons iced water
1 egg yolk beaten with 1 tablespoon water for glaze

Filling:
2 (5-oz.) cans white chunk chicken, well-drained
2 tablespoons butter or margarine, melted
2 tablespoons lemon juice
2 (3-oz.) pkgs. cream cheese, room temperature
1 egg, beaten
Salt
Freshly ground pepper
1 (4-oz.) jar sliced pimentos, drained
1 (2-oz.) jar capers, drained, coarsely chopped
1/3 cup chopped fresh parsley

To garnish:
Green-onion curls

1. To make pastry, in a medium bowl, combine flour, lemon peel and salt. With a pastry blender or 2 knives, cut in butter or margarine until mixture resembles coarse crumbs. Sprinkle with 3 tablespoons water; toss with a fork until mixture holds together, adding additional water if necessary. Gather dough into a flattened ball. Wrap in plastic wrap or waxed paper; refrigerate 30 minutes.
2. Preheat oven to 400F (205C). Lightly grease a 7" x 3" or 8" x 4" loaf pan. On a lightly floured surface, roll out 3/4 of chilled dough to a rectangle large enough to line loaf pan. Use rolled dough to line greased loaf pan.
3. To make filling, place chicken in a medium bowl; flake with a fork. Stir in butter or margarine. In a medium bowl, beat lemon juice, cream cheese, egg, salt and pepper until combined. Stir cheese mixture into chicken mixture.
4. Scatter pimentos in bottom of pastry-lined pan. Top with capers. Spoon 1/2 of chicken mixture over capers; spread with back of spoon. Sprinkle parsley over chicken. Top with remaining chicken mixture. Fold pastry edges over chicken mixture.
5. On a lightly floured board, roll out remaining 1/4 of pastry to make top crust. Cover loaf with rolled dough. Crimp and flute edges. Decorate top with pastry trimmings, if desired. Brush with egg glaze.
6. Bake in preheated oven 50 to 55 minutes or until pastry is golden brown. Cool completely in pan on a wire rack. Invert pan on a serving plate; refrigerate until served. To serve, cut into slices; garnish with green-onion curls. Makes 6 to 8 servings.

Cheesy Onion Ring

Pastry:
2 cups all-purpose flour
1 teaspoon salt
3/4 cup butter or margarine
1 egg yolk
1/4 cup iced water
1 egg yolk beaten with 1 tablespoon water for glaze
Poppy seeds or sesame seeds

Filling:
2 cups shredded sharp Cheddar cheese (8 oz.)
1 cup finely chopped onions
1/2 teaspoon Italian seasoning
3 tablespoons mustard-pickle relish

To garnish:
Curly endive leaves

Left to right: Creamy Chicken Loaf en Croûte, Cheesy Onion Ring

1. To make pastry, in a medium bowl, combine flour and salt. With a pastry blender or 2 knives, cut in butter or margarine until mixture resembles coarse crumbs. In a small bowl, beat egg yolk and water until blended. Sprinkle over flour; toss with a fork until mixture holds together. Gather dough into a flattened ball. Wrap in plastic wrap or waxed paper; refrigerate 30 minutes.

2. Preheat oven to 400F (205C). Grease a baking sheet.

3. To make filling, in a medium bowl, combine cheese, onions, Italian seasoning and pickle relish.

4. On a lightly floured surface, roll out pastry to a 16" x 12" rectangle. Spread cheese filling over pastry to within 1/2 inch of edges. Brush 1 long edge of pastry with egg glaze. Roll up, jelly-roll style, starting from long unglazed edge. Press seam to seal. Lift filled roll carefully; place roll, seam-side down, on greased baking sheet.

5. Cut roll at 1-1/2-inch intervals with scissors, cutting almost through to opposite side of roll. Shape roll into a ring. Brush ends with glaze; press firmly to seal. Raise each cut section carefully; tilt back slightly to expose filling. Brush ring all over with egg glaze; sprinkle with poppy seeds or sesame seeds.

6. Bake in preheated oven 30 to 35 minutes or until golden brown. Cool on baking sheet on a wire rack 10 minutes. Slide ring off baking sheet carefully; cool on rack. Fill center with endive; serve warm. Makes 6 to 8 servings.

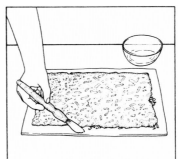

1/Brush 1 long edge of pastry with egg glaze.

2/Roll up, jelly-roll style, starting from long unglazed edge.

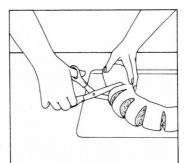

3/Cut roll at 1-1/2-inch intervals with scissors, cutting almost through to opposite side of roll.

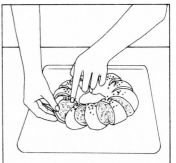

4/Raise each cut section carefully; tilt back slightly to expose filling.

Farmhouse Pâté

6 bacon slices
6 tablespoons butter or margarine
8 oz. pork liver, chopped
8 oz. salt pork, blanched, chopped
1 large onion, chopped
1 garlic clove, crushed
3 tablespoons all-purpose flour
1/2 cup milk
1/2 cup dry wine or apple cider
Salt
Freshly ground pepper
4 bay leaves
6 allspice berries

1. Preheat oven to 350F (175C). Grease a 1-quart terrine. Line bottom and sides of greased terrine with bacon.
2. Melt 1/4 cup butter or margarine in a large skillet. Add liver, salt pork, onion and garlic; cook 10 minutes. In a blender or food processor fitted with a steel blade, process liver mixture until smooth.
3. Melt remaining 2 tablespoons butter or margarine in a medium saucepan. Stir in flour; cook 1 minute, stirring. Gradually stir in milk and wine or cider. Bring to a boil; stirring constantly, cook 3 minutes. Season with salt and pepper. Stir into liver mixture. Spoon into terrine, leveling surface.
4. Top with bay leaves and allspice berries. Cover with buttered foil or a lid; place in a roasting pan. Add enough boiling water to roasting pan to come halfway up sides of terrine.
5. Bake in preheated oven 1 hour or until firm to the touch. Cool at room temperature 30 minutes. Cover and refrigerate until chilled. Pâté can be refrigerated up to 2 days or frozen up to 1 month. Thaw overnight in refrigerator before serving. Makes 8 servings.

Left to right: Stuffed French Bread, Farmhouse Pâté

Mushroom Quiche

Pastry:
1-1/2 cups all-purpose flour
1/2 teaspoon salt
1/2 cup vegetable shortening
3 to 4 tablespoons iced water

Filling:
2 tablespoons butter or margarine
1 small onion, chopped
8 oz. mushrooms, sliced (about 3-1/4 cups)
1/2 cup plain yogurt
1/2 cup whipping cream
3 eggs, beaten
2 teaspoons Italian seasoning
2 teaspoons chopped chives or chopped
   green-onion tops
Salt
Freshly ground pepper

1. To make pastry, in a medium bowl, combine flour and salt. With a pastry blender or 2 knives, cut in shortening until mixture resembles coarse crumbs. Sprinkle with 3 tablespoons iced water; toss with a fork until mixture holds together, adding additional water if necessary. Gather dough into a flattened ball. Wrap in plastic wrap or waxed paper; refrigerate 30 minutes.
2. Preheat oven to 400F (205C). On a lightly floured board, roll out pastry to an 11-inch circle. Use to line a 9- or 10-inch pie pan or quiche pan. Crimp and flute pastry edge; prick bottom lightly with a fork. Line pastry with foil; fill with pie weights or dried beans.
3. Bake in preheated oven 15 minutes. Remove foil and pie weights or beans; bake 5 to 8 minutes or until golden. Set aside to cool. Reduce oven temperature to 375F (190C).
4. To make filling, melt butter or margarine in a medium saucepan. Add onion; cook about 5 minutes or until softened. Add mushrooms; cook 3 minutes. Set aside.
5. In a small bowl, combine yogurt, cream and eggs. Stir into mushroom mixture. Stir in Italian seasoning, chives or onion tops, salt and pepper. Pour mushroom mixture into cooled pastry shell.
6. Bake in preheated oven 35 minutes or until set. Serve hot or cold, cut into wedges. Makes 4 to 6 servings.

Stuffed French Bread

1 large French-bread loaf
2 tablespoons butter or margarine, room temperature
Coleslaw:
1/4 head cabbage, shredded
1/2 small onion, finely chopped
1 small carrot, grated
1 celery stalk, chopped
3 tablespoons raisins
2 tablespoons coarsely chopped walnuts
3 to 4 tablespoons mayonnaise
Filling:
2 lettuce leaves, shredded
3 bologna slices, rolled
3 salami slices, rolled into cornets
2 oz. smoked cheese, sliced
2 oz. blue cheese, sliced
1 hard-cooked egg, sliced
1 large tomato, sliced

1. Split loaf in half horizontally. Thinly spread butter or margarine on cut sides of loaf.
2. To make coleslaw, in a medium bowl, combine cabbage, onion, carrot, celery, raisins and walnuts. Stir in enough mayonnaise to bind ingredients.
3. Spread coleslaw along length of bottom half of loaf; top with lettuce, bologna, salami, smoked cheese, blue cheese, hard-cooked egg and tomato, arranging attractively.
4. Press loaf halves firmly together; cut vertically into 3 sections to serve. Makes 3 servings.

Variation
For an Oriental-flavored coleslaw, substitute shredded Chinese cabbage for regular cabbage, bean sprouts for celery and water chestnuts for onions. Continue as above.

Left to right: Ham & Smoked-Cheese Flan, Spanish Vegetable & Ham Quiche

Ham & Smoked-Cheese Flan

Pastry:
1-1/2 cups all-purpose flour
1/2 teaspoon salt
1/2 cup vegetable shortening
3 to 4 tablespoons iced water

Filling:
1 cup chopped cooked ham (about 4 oz.)
1 cup shredded smoked cheese (4 oz.)
3 eggs, beaten
1/2 cup half and half
Pinch of salt
1/4 teaspoon freshly grated nutmeg

To garnish:
3 tomatoes, cut into wedges

1. To make pastry, in a medium bowl, combine flour and salt. With a pastry blender or 2 knives, cut in shortening until mixture resembles coarse crumbs. Sprinkle with 3 tablespoons iced water; toss with a fork until mixture holds together, adding additional water if necessary. Gather dough into a flattened ball. Wrap in plastic wrap or waxed paper; refrigerate 30 minutes.
2. Preheat oven to 400F (205C). On a lightly floured board, roll out pastry to an 11-inch circle. Use to line a 9- or 10-inch pie pan or quiche pan. Crimp and flute pastry edge; prick bottom lightly with a fork. Line pastry with foil; fill with pie weights or dried beans.
3. Bake in preheated oven 15 minutes. Remove foil and pie weights or beans; bake 5 to 8 minutes or until golden. Set aside to cool. Reduce oven temperature to 375F (190C).
4. Sprinkle ham and cheese over bottom of cooled pastry shell. In a medium bowl, combine eggs, half and half, salt and nutmeg; carefully pour over ham and cheese.
5. Bake in preheated oven 35 minutes or until set. Serve flan warm or cold. Garnish with tomato wedges. Makes to 6 servings.

Quiche Lorraine

Pastry:
1-1/2 cups all-purpose flour
1/2 teaspoon salt
1/2 cup vegetable shortening
3 to 4 tablespoons iced water

Filling:
1/2 lb. bacon, crisp-cooked, crumbled
1-1/2 cups grated Swiss or Gruyère cheese (6 oz.)
3 eggs
1-1/2 cups half and half
1/4 teaspoon freshly grated nutmeg
Salt
Freshly ground pepper

1. To make pastry, in a medium bowl, combine flour and salt. With a pastry blender or 2 knives, cut in shortening until mixture resembles coarse crumbs. Sprinkle with 3 tablespoons iced water; toss with a fork until mixture holds together, adding additional water if necessary. Gather dough into a flattened ball. Wrap in plastic wrap or waxed paper; refrigerate 30 minutes.
2. Preheat oven to 400F (205C). On a lightly floured board, roll out pastry to an 11-inch circle. Use to line a 9- or 10-inch pie pan or quiche pan. Crimp and flute pastry edge; prick bottom lightly with a fork. Line pastry with foil; fill with pie weights or dried beans.
3. Bake in preheated oven 15 minutes. Remove foil and pie weights or beans; bake 5 to 8 minutes or until golden. Set aside to cool. Reduce oven temperature to 375F (190C).
4. Scatter bacon in bottom of cooled pastry shell. Sprinkle 1/2 of cheese over bacon.
5. In a medium bowl, beat eggs, half and half, nutmeg, salt and pepper until blended. Carefully pour into pastry shell. Sprinkle remaining 3/4 cup cheese on top.
6. Bake in preheated oven 35 to 45 minutes or until puffed and top is golden brown.
7. Cool in pan on a wire rack 15 minutes. Serve warm. Makes 6 servings.

Variation
Spinach Quiche: Omit bacon. Thaw and drain 1 (10-ounce) package frozen chopped spinach. Heat 2 tablespoons butter or margarine in a medium skillet. Slice 1 bunch green onions; add to skillet. Cook 2 to 3 minutes. Stir in spinach; cook 1 minute. Scatter 3/4 cup cheese in bottom of cooled pastry shell. Spoon spinach mixture over cheese. Continue with step 5.

Spanish Vegetable & Ham Quiche

Pastry:
1-1/2 cups all-purpose flour
1/2 teaspoon salt
1/2 cup vegetable shortening
3 to 4 tablespoons iced water

Filling:
2 tablespoons butter or margarine
1 small red bell pepper, sliced
1 small green bell pepper, sliced
5 oz. mushrooms, sliced (about 2 cups)
1 small zucchini, sliced
1 cup chopped cooked ham (about 4 oz.)
3 eggs
1-1/4 cups half and half
1/4 cup grated Parmesan cheese (3/4 oz.)
1/2 teaspoon ground cumin
Salt
Freshly ground black pepper

1. To make pastry, in a medium bowl, combine flour and salt. With a pastry blender or 2 knives, cut in shortening until mixture resembles coarse crumbs. Sprinkle with 3 tablespoons iced water; toss with a fork until mixture holds together, adding additional water if necessary. Gather dough into a flattened ball. Wrap in plastic wrap or waxed paper; refrigerate 30 minutes.
2. Preheat oven to 400F (205C). On a lightly floured board, roll out pastry to an 11-inch circle. Use to line a 9- or 10-inch pie pan or quiche pan. Crimp and flute pastry edge; prick bottom lightly with a fork. Line pastry with foil; fill with pie weights or dried beans.
3. Bake in preheated oven 15 minutes. Remove foil and pie weights or beans; bake 5 to 8 minutes or until golden. Set aside to cool. Reduce oven temperature to 375F (190C).
4. To make filling, melt butter or margarine in a medium skillet. Add bell peppers, mushrooms and zucchini; sauté 5 to 6 minutes or until tender.
5. Scatter ham in bottom of cooled pastry shell. Arrange cooked vegetables over ham. In a medium bowl, beat eggs, half and half, cheese, cumin, salt and black pepper until blended. Carefully pour egg mixture over vegetable mixture.
6. Bake in preheated oven 40 to 45 minutes or until center is set and top is golden brown. Remove from oven; cool slightly. Serve warm or cold. Makes 4 to 6 servings.

Pork with Orange & Ginger

2 tablespoons butter or margarine
1 lb. pork tenderloin, sliced into 1/4-inch rounds
Salt
Freshly ground pepper
1 teaspoon grated gingerroot
1 tablespoon brown sugar
1 tablespoon orange juice
1 tablespoon cider vinegar
4 green onions, finely chopped

To garnish:
Orange peel, cut in julienne strips

This dish is delicious served with small onions in a cream sauce.

1. Melt butter or margarine in a large skillet. Add pork. Season with salt and pepper. Brown pork rounds quickly on both sides 6 to 8 minutes or until golden brown and tender. Remove with a slotted spoon; arrange on a warmed serving plate. Keep warm.
2. Stir gingerroot, brown sugar, orange juice, vinegar and green onions into pan juices. Heat until mixture forms a syrupy glaze.
3. Spoon glaze over pork; garnish with orange peel. Makes 4 servings.

Variation
Pork with Apricots & Cinnamon: Substitute 1 tablespoon apricot jam and a pinch of ground cinnamon for grated gingerroot. Soak 2 tablespoons finely chopped dried apricots in water 30 minutes; substitute these for orange peel.

Orange- & Honey-Glazed Game Hens

3 tablespoons honey
1 tablespoon Dijon-style mustard
1 tablespoon vegetable oil
1 cup orange juice
3 tablespoons tomato paste
Grated peel of 1 orange
1 teaspoon prepared horseradish
1 tablespoon lemon juice
1/2 teaspoon ground ginger
Salt
Freshly ground pepper
4 game hens, trussed

1. Preheat oven to 375F (190C). In a medium saucepan combine honey, mustard, oil, orange juice, tomato paste, orange peel, horseradish, lemon juice, ginger, salt and pepper. Boil over medium heat about 10 minutes or until syrupy.
2. Arrange hens in a roasting pan; brush generously with orange-and-honey glaze.
3. Roast in preheated oven 45 minutes or until tender and golden brown, basting hens frequently with glaze. If hens brown too quickly, cover with foil during last part of cooking. Hens are done when juices run clear when pierced with a sharp knife between breast and thigh.
4. Remove hens from pan; place on a warmed serving dish. Add remaining glaze to pan; boil until reduced to a thick syrupy consistency.
5. Spoon over hens; serve hot. Garnish with watercress sprigs. Makes 4 large servings.

Variation
Pineapple- & Honey-Glazed Game Hens: Substitute unsweetened pineapple juice for orange juice and grated peel of 1 lemon for orange peel.

Left to right: Pork with Orange & Ginger, Orange- & Honey-Glazed Game Hen

Left to right: Pork Chops with Spicy Mustard Sauce, Veal with Tomato Sauce

Pork Chops with Spicy Mustard Sauce

---

1 tablespoon vegetable oil
4 pork chops (about 6 oz. each)
1/4 cup prepared coarse mustard
1/2 teaspoon freshly grated nutmeg
1 cup dry white wine or chicken stock
Salt
Freshly ground pepper
1/2 cup whipping cream

To garnish:
2 tablespoon chopped fresh parsley

---

1. Heat oil in a deep skillet with a lid. Add pork chops; brown quickly on both sides. Remove with tongs; keep warm.
2. Stir mustard, nutmeg, wine or stock, salt and pepper into fat remaining in skillet. Return chops to skillet. Cover skillet; simmer 20 minutes.
3. Stir in cream; simmer until sauce is reduced and thickened, stirring gently.
4. Sprinkle with chopped parsley. Serve hot with green noodles and a crisp salad. Makes 4 servings.

Veal with Tomato Sauce

2 tablespoons butter or margarine
1 tablespoon vegetable oil
4 thinly sliced veal cutlets (about 4 oz. each)
Salt
Freshly ground pepper
1 onion, finely chopped
2 teaspoons all-purpose flour
1 cup chicken stock
2 tablespoons dry red wine
2 teaspoons tomato paste
1 teaspoon Italian seasoning
1 bay leaf
1 (10-oz.) pkg. frozen spinach
1/2 teaspoon freshly grated nutmeg
7 oz. Camembert cheese

Fresh Tomato Sauce:
1 tablespoon butter or margarine
1 garlic clove, crushed
3 to 4 tomatoes, peeled, seeded, chopped
1/4 teaspoon finely chopped fresh basil, if desired

1. Heat butter or margarine and oil in a large skillet. Season veal with salt and pepper; add seasoned veal to skillet; brown quickly on both sides. Remove with tongs; keep warm.
2. Add onion to fat remaining in skillet; cook until softened. Stir in flour; cook 1 minute, stirring.
3. Gradually stir in stock, wine and tomato paste to make a smooth sauce. Stir in Italian seasoning, bay leaf, salt and pepper. Add veal; simmer about 10 minutes or until veal is tender.
4. Meanwhile, cook spinach according to package directions. Drain; stir in nutmeg. Place seasoned spinach around edge of a flameproof serving dish; keep warm.
5. To make tomato sauce, melt butter or margarine in a medium saucepan. Add garlic and tomatoes; simmer 5 minutes. Add basil, if desired.
6. Preheat broiler. Remove veal from onion sauce; place veal inside spinach ring. Spread veal with tomato sauce.
7. Cut cheese into 4 slices, cutting into heart shapes, if desired. Arrange cheese slices on veal. Broil under preheated broiler until cheese melts.
8. Serve immediately; serve onion sauce separately. Makes 4 servings.

Spicy Lamb en Papillote

1/4 cup butter or margarine
6 lamb loin chops
2 onions, sliced
2 garlic cloves, crushed
1 teaspoon ground ginger
1 teaspoon ground allspice
1 teaspoon dried rosemary
2 tablespoons honey
Salt
Freshly ground pepper

To garnish:
Fresh rosemary sprigs
Tomato slices

1. Preheat oven to 375F (190C). Melt butter or margarine in a large skillet. Add lamb chops; brown quickly on both sides. Remove from skillet with a slotted spoon; set aside.
2. Add onion and garlic to skillet; sauté 3 minutes.
3. Stir in ginger, allspice and rosemary. Cook 1 minute.
4. Stir in honey; season with salt and pepper. Cook 1 minute.
5. Cut 6 foil squares, making each large enough to completely cover a lamb chop. Fold squares in half diagonally. Trim each foil triangle to a semicircle. Open out foil; place a chop on 1 side of opened-out foil. Top each chop with 1/4 of onion mixture. Loosely fold foil to enclose chops and topping. Seal edges by crimping into small pleats, finishing with a little twist at end; see below. Place papillotes on a baking sheet.
6. Bake in preheated oven 45 to 50 minutes or until lamb is tender. Garnish with rosemary sprigs and tomato. Makes 6 servings.

1/Trim each foil triangle to a semicircle.

2/Seal edges by crimping into small pleats, finishing with a little twist at end.

Roast Chicken

1/4 cup regular rolled oats
1 cup fresh bread crumbs
1 small onion, finely chopped
3/4 cup finely chopped cooked ham (3 oz.)
2 celery stalks, finely chopped
1 tablespoon chopped fresh parsley
1/2 teaspoon dried leaf thyme
Salt
Freshly ground pepper
1 egg, beaten
1 (4-lb.) roasting chicken
2 tablespoons butter or margarine

1. Preheat oven to 375F (190C). In a small bowl, combine rolled oats, bread crumbs, onion, ham, celery, parsley, thyme, salt and pepper. Stir in egg.
2. Using your hands, from neck end, carefully lift skin from chicken breast taking care not to puncture skin. Push stuffing under breast skin. Carefully pull skin over stuffing; secure to chicken back with wooden picks or string. Truss chicken.
3. Place stuffed chicken in a roasting pan; dot with butter or margarine. Season with salt and pepper.
4. Bake in preheated oven 1-1/2 to 2 hours or until juices run clear when chicken is pierced between breast and thigh with a sharp knife.
5. Serve roasted chicken hot or cold. If chicken is served cold, remove stuffing and refrigerate separately. Makes 6 servings.

Left to right: Steak with Green-Peppercorn Sauce, Duck with Plum Sauce

Steaks with Green-Peppercorn Sauce

4 beef-loin tenderloin steaks (about 5 oz. each)
Salt
Freshly ground pepper
1/4 cup butter or margarine
2 tablespoons brandy
1/2 cup whipping cream
2 tablespoons green peppercorns

To garnish:
Watercress sprigs

1. Season steaks with salt and pepper.
2. Melt butter or margarine in a large skillet. Add steaks; sauté over medium-high heat 3 to 5 minutes on each side until browned, depending of degree of doneness desired.
3. Pour brandy over steaks; heat until warmed. Ignite warm brandy. When flames die down, remove steaks from skillet with tongs. Place on a warmed serving dish.
4. Add cream and peppercorns to pan; cook 1 minute or until slightly thickened.
5. Spoon sauce over steaks; garnish with watercress sprigs. Serve with cooked fresh green beans or other green vegetable. Makes 4 servings.

Duck with Plum Sauce

1 (20-oz.) can plums
2 tablespoons ketchup
2 tablespoons molasses
1 tablespoon wine vinegar
1 teaspoon prepared mustard
1-1/2 teaspoons five-spice powder
1 garlic clove, crushed
Salt
Freshly ground pepper
4 duck quarters or 1 (5-lb.) oven-ready duck, quartered

1. Preheat oven to 375F (190C). Drain plums, reserving syrup. Remove and discard plum pits. In a blender or food processor fitted with a steel blade, process plums, ketchup, molasses, vinegar, mustard, five-spice powder, garlic, salt and pepper until smooth. Or, combine ingredients in a medium bowl. Press through a fine sieve.
2. Add 3 tablespoons reserved syrup or enough syrup to make puree a good consistency for basting.
3. Prick duck all over to allow excess fat to escape during roasting. Place duck in a roasting pan; brush generously with plum sauce.
4. Roast in preheated oven about 1-1/2 hours or until crisp and golden, basting frequently with plum sauce. Juices should run clear when duck is pierced with a sharp knife between breast and thigh. Serve hot or cold with a crisp salad. If desired, in a medium saucepan, boil remaining basting sauce 3 minutes; spoon over roasted duck. Makes 4 servings.

Ham & Mushroom Gougère

1 tablespoon vegetable oil
1 onion, chopped
4 oz. mushrooms, sliced (about 1-3/4 cups)
2 cups chopped cooked ham (about 8 oz.)
Freshly ground pepper
6 tablespoons butter or margarine
3/4 cup water
3/4 cup all-purpose flour
3 eggs
2 tablespoons fresh bread crumbs
3/4 cup shredded Cheddar cheese (3 oz.)
1 tablespoon chopped fresh chives

1. Preheat oven to 425F (220C). Grease an oval 12" x 7" x 3" baking dish. Heat oil in a medium skillet. Add onion and mushrooms; cook about 5 minutes or until softened. Add ham and pepper. Set aside.
2. Heat butter or margarine and water in a medium, heavy saucepan until mixture boils. Add flour, all at once. With a wooden spoon, beat over medium heat until mixture is smooth and forms a ball that leaves side of saucepan.
3. Cool slightly; beat in eggs, 1 at a time, beating well after each addition.
4. Spread 1/2 of this choux paste over base of greased dish; spoon remaining choux paste around edge of dish. The layer of choux paste will not be very thick. Spoon ham mixture into center. Sprinkle evenly with bread crumbs.
5. Bake in preheated oven 25 minutes or until puffed and golden brown. Sprinkle ham mixture with cheese; bake 5 to 10 minutes or until cheese melts and dough is firm.
6. Sprinkle with chives; serve immediately. Makes 4 servings.

Variation
For two people, halve quantities, using two eggs; reduce cooking time to about 25 minutes.

Pasta with Creamy Ham & Cheese Sauce

8 oz. pasta shells (about 2 cups)
Salt
2 tablespoons butter or margarine
4 oz. mushrooms, sliced (about 1-3/4 cups)
1-1/2 cups chopped cooked ham (about 6 oz.)
1/2 cup whipping cream
1-1/2 cups shredded Cheddar cheese (6 oz.)
Freshly ground pepper
1 tablespoon chopped fresh parsley

To garnish:
6 to 8 black olives
2 tablespoons grated Parmesan cheese

1. Cook pasta shells in a large saucepan of salted boiling water according to package directions until tender. Do not overcook. Drain thoroughly.
2. Preheat oven to 350F (175C). Melt butter or margarine in a large saucepan. Add mushrooms and ham; cook about 5 minutes or until mushrooms are softened. Add drained pasta; toss over low heat to warm through.
3. In a medium bowl, combine cream, cheese, salt, pepper and parsley. Stir into pasta mixture; stir over low heat until pasta is coated and sauce is slightly thickened.
4. Spoon into a warmed serving dish. Garnish with black olives; sprinkle with Parmesan cheese. Serve hot with a green salad. Makes 4 servings.

Mushroom Puffs

1/2 (17-1/4-oz.) pkg. frozen puff pastry
    (1 sheet), thawed
6 oz. mushrooms, chopped (about 2-1/2 cups)
Lemon juice
2 teaspoons finely chopped fresh parsley
1 teaspoon chopped chives
Vegetable oil for deep-frying

Blue-Cheese Sauce:
4 oz. blue cheese, crumbled
2/3 cup plain yogurt or dairy sour cream
2 tablespoons milk
1 tablespoon chopped fresh chives
Salt
White pepper

To garnish:
Lemon slices
Fresh parsley sprigs

1. Unfold pastry; lay flat on a lightly floured surface. With a lightly floured rolling pin, roll out pastry to a 12-inch square. Cut into 16 (3-inch) squares.
2. In a medium bowl, combine mushrooms, lemon juice, parsley and chives. Brush edges of each pastry square lightly with water. Spoon 1 tablespoon mushroom mixture on center of 1/2 of pastry squares. Top each with 1 of remaining pastry squares. Pinch edges to seal tightly.
3. Heat oil in a deep saucepan or deep-fat fryer to 350F (175C) or until a 1-inch bread cube turns golden brown in 65 seconds. Drop 3 to 4 mushroom parcels into hot oil; fry 2 to 3 minutes. Turn parcels over; fry 2 to 3 minutes or until golden brown. Remove with a slotted spoon; drain on paper towels. Keep warm. Repeat with remaining mushroom parcels.
4. To make sauce, in a blender, process cheese, yogurt or sour cream and milk until smooth. Add chives; process until finely chopped. Season with salt and white pepper. Spoon sauce into a small serving bowl.
5. Arrange mushroom puffs on a warmed serving plate. Garnish with lemon slices and parsley sprigs. Serve warm with sauce. Makes 8 servings of 2 puffs each.

Left to right: Mushroom Puffs with Blue-Cheese Sauce, Ham & Mushroom Gougère

Bobotie

2 tablespoons butter or margarine
1 onion, finely chopped
1 apple, peeled, cored, finely chopped
1 tablespoon mild curry powder
1 tablespoon apricot jam or mango chutney
1 large bread slice, crusts removed
2 to 3 tablespoons milk
1-1/2 lb. cooked ground lamb
3 tablespoons raisins
1 tablespoon lemon juice
Salt
Freshly ground pepper
2 eggs, beaten
3/4 cup milk
1/4 cup sliced almonds

Although Malay in origin, Bobotie is one of South Africa's typical informal dishes. It consists of curried lamb with a savory custard topping. Bobotie is a perfect make-ahead dish since it needs little last-minute attention.

1. Preheat oven to 350F (175C). Melt butter or margarine in a medium saucepan. Add onion and apple; cook about 5 minutes or until softened.
2. Stir in curry powder; cook 2 minutes. Stir in jam or chutney; cook 1 minute. Set aside.
3. Meanwhile, soak bread in 2 to 3 tablespoons milk. Squeeze to remove excess milk. In a medium bowl, combine lamb, onion mixture, raisins, lemon juice, salt and pepper. Place in a 1-1/2 quart casserole; smooth surface.
4. Beat eggs with 3/4 cup milk, salt and pepper. Pour through a strainer over meat mixture. Sprinkle with almonds.
5. Bake in preheated oven 45 minutes or until topping is set and golden. Serve hot with cooked rice, sliced onions, sliced tomatoes, shredded coconut, chutney and poppadums. For information about poppadums, see comments in recipe for Tropical Curried-Chicken Salad, page 38. Makes 4 servings.

Toad-in-the-Hole with Tomato Sauce

1 lb. bulk pork sausage
2 teaspoons Italian seasoning.
1 onion, finely chopped
3 tablespoons vegetable oil
1 cup all-purpose flour
Salt
2 eggs
1 cup milk

Chunky Tomato Sauce:
1 onion, finely chopped
1 garlic clove, crushed
1 (1-lb.) can tomatoes with juice, chopped
1 (6-oz.) can tomato paste
1/4 cup red wine, beef stock or tomato juice
1 tablespoon brown sugar
1 teaspoon Worcestershire sauce
1/2 teaspoon dried leaf oregano
1/2 teaspoon dried leaf basil
Salt
Freshly ground pepper

To garnish:
Finely chopped fresh parsley

1. Preheat oven to 400F (205C). In a medium bowl, combine sausage, Italian seasoning and onion. Shape mixture into 12 equal balls. Heat 1 tablespoon oil in a large skillet; add sausage balls; brown on all sides. Remove with a slotted spoon; drain on paper towels.
2. In a medium bowl, combine flour and a pinch of salt. Make a well in center; stir in eggs to make a thick paste. Gradually stir in milk. Beat to make a smooth batter.
3. Place remaining 2 tablespoons oil in a 13" x 9" baking pan or 2 (9-inch) round pans. Add browned sausage balls, spacing them evenly.
4. Bake in preheated oven 10 minutes or until oil sizzles. Pour batter around sausage balls; bake 40 minutes or until puffed and golden brown.
5. While mixture is baking, make sauce. To make sauce, add onion to fat remaining in skillet. Cook over medium heat about 5 minutes or until softened. Stir in remaining sauce ingredients. Bring to a boil. Reduce heat; simmer 30 to 40 minutes or until slightly thickened.
6. Serve baked toad-in-the-hole with tomato sauce. Makes 4 servings.

Left to right: Toad-in-the-Hole with Tomato Sauce,
Soufflé Surprise

Soufflé Surprises

4 small rolls
5 tablespoons butter or margarine, room temperature
6 to 8 thin slices cooked ham
5 tablespoons all-purpose flour
3/4 cup milk
2 small eggs, separated
1/2 cup shredded Gruyère cheese (2 oz.)
Salt
Freshly ground pepper
1 teaspoon Italian seasoning
1 small canned pimento, finely chopped

1. Cut top off each roll; scoop out soft bread from inside, reserving for another use.
2. Using 2 tablespoons butter or margarine, coat outside of each roll. Wrap rolls in foil to protect them from too much heat, leaving tops exposed.
3. Line insides of scooped-out roll with ham slices, allowing slices to show above roll tops.
4. Preheat oven to 375F (190C). Melt remaining 3 tablespoons butter or margarine in a medium saucepan. Stir in flour; cook 1 minute, stirring. Gradually stir in milk, blending well. Bring to a boil; cook 2 to 3 minutes, stirring. Remove from heat; cool slightly.
5. Stir egg yolks, cheese, salt, pepper, Italian seasoning and pimento into sauce mixture, blending well.
6. In a medium bowl, beat egg whites until stiff but not dry. Fold beaten egg whites into egg-yolk mixture. Spoon soufflé mixture into ham-lined rolls. Place filled rolls on a baking sheet.
7. Bake in preheated oven 25 to 30 minutes or until puffed and golden brown. Remove foil. Serve immediately. Makes 2 to 4 servings.

Sausage Tarts

2 tablespoons butter or margarine
1 tablespoon vegetable oil
20 pearl onions
8 oz. breakfast sausages, cut into 1-inch pieces
8 oz. beef for stew, cut into 1-inch pieces
1 tablespoon all-purpose flour
1 cup beef stock
3/4 cup dry red wine
8 oz. small mushrooms
1 teaspoon chopped fresh thyme
1 teaspoon prepared horseradish
Salt
Freshly ground pepper
1 (17-1/4-oz.) pkg. frozen puff pastry, thawed
1 egg, beaten

1. Heat butter or margarine and oil in a large saucepan. Add onions; cook until softened. Add sausages and beef cubes; cook about 10 minutes or until lightly browned. Remove with a slotted spoon; set aside.
2. Stir flour into fat remaining in pan; cook 1 minute, stirring. Gradually stir in stock and wine. Add sausage mixture, mushrooms, thyme, horseradish, salt and pepper. Cover and simmer over low heat 15 to 20 minutes. Spoon into 4 (1-1/2- to 2-cup) casseroles; cool slightly.
3. Preheat oven to 400F (205C). On a lightly floured surface, roll out 1 pastry sheet at a time; cut into 2 rounds, each about 1-1/2 inches larger than a casserole. Place pastry rounds over filling in casseroles. Trim, seal and flute edges. Use pastry trimmings for decorations, if desired. Brush with beaten egg to glaze.
4. Bake in preheated oven 20 minutes or until crust puffs and is golden brown. Serve hot. Makes 4 servings.

Japanese-Style Kidneys

1/4 cup soy sauce
3 tablespoons dry sherry
2 tablespoons honey
1 cup beef stock
1 garlic clove, crushed
Pinch of five-spice powder
12 lambs' kidneys, halved, cored
3 tablespoons all-purpose flour
Salt
Freshly ground pepper
3 tablespoons butter or margarine
1 tablespoon cornstarch
Water

To serve:
Hot cooked rice

To garnish:
Green-onion curls
Carrot shapes

1. In a medium bowl, combine soy sauce, sherry, honey, stock, garlic and five-spice powder. Add kidneys, tossing well to coat. Cover and marinate 30 minutes.
2. Remove marinated kidneys with a slotted spoon; pat dry with paper towels. Reserve marinade. In a plastic bag, combine flour, salt and pepper. Add kidneys; shake to coat.
3. Melt butter or margarine in a deep skillet. Add coated kidneys; cook over medium heat 5 minutes. Remove with a slotted spoon; keep warm.
4. Add marinade to skillet; bring to a boil, stirring constantly. In a small bowl, blend cornstarch with a little water; stir into sauce. Cook until slightly thickened, stirring constantly.
5. Add cooked kidneys to sauce; season with salt and pepper. Cook 1 to 2 minutes or until kidneys are heated through. To serve, spoon rice in a ring around a serving plate; spoon kidney mixture into center of rice. Garnish with onion curls and carrots. Makes 4 servings.

To make *green-onion curls*, trim off most of the dark-green top. Thinly slice from remaining green top almost to root end of onion. Place in iced water until ends curl.

To make *vegetable shapes*, peel carrots, turnips or rutabagas. Slice crosswise into thin slices; cut out shapes with a canapé cutter or sharp knife. Traditional shapes include hearts, fish, moons and flowers.

Calves' Liver with Sage

1/4 cup butter or margarine
1 tablespoon grated onion
4 large thin slices calves' liver (about 3-1/2 oz. each)
3 tablespoons chopped fresh sage
Salt
Freshly ground pepper
1/4 cup vegetable oil
4 cups diced, peeled potatoes (about 1-1/2 lb.)
2 tablespoons dry sherry or beef stock

To garnish:
1 tablespoon chopped fresh parsley, if desired
Fresh sage sprigs

1. Melt butter or margarine in a large skillet. Add onion; cook about 2 minutes or until softened. Add liver; cook over low heat about 3 minutes or until browned on 1 side. Turn over; sprinkle generously with sage, salt and pepper; cook about 2 minutes or until browned on remaining side.
2. Meanwhile, in a deep skillet, heat oil over medium heat until hot. Add potatoes; sauté about 10 minutes or until golden, crisp and tender, stirring frequently. Drain on paper towels. Sprinkle with salt.
3. Remove cooked liver from skillet with tongs; arrange on a warmed serving plate with cooked potatoes.
4. Stir sherry or stock into liver pan juices. Cook 1 minute to reduce slightly; pour over cooked liver. Sprinkle liver with chopped parsley, if desired. Garnish with sage leaves. Serve immediately. Makes 4 servings.

Left to right: Calves' Liver with Sage, Japanese-Style Kidneys

Trout with Tarragon

4 trout, ready to cook
1/2 cup dry white wine
2 tablespoons water
1 tablespoon finely chopped onion
1 lemon, thinly sliced
2 tablespoons chopped fresh parsley
2 tablespoons chopped fresh tarragon
1/2 cup whipping cream
Salt
Freshly ground pepper

---

1. Place trout in a large skillet with a lid. Add wine, water, onion, lemon and 1/2 of parsley and tarragon. Bring to a simmer. Cover and poach 10 to 12 minutes or until trout tests done.
2. Remove trout and lemon slices; arrange decoratively on a warmed serving plate; keep warm.
3. Add cream to skillet; increase heat. Cook until thickened, stirring constantly; season with salt and pepper. Spoon sauce over trout.
4. Sprinkle with remaining parsley and tarragon. Makes 4 servings.

Honey-Baked Fish

2 mackerel or other fish (about 1 lb. each), ready to cook
2 tablespoons honey
1 carrot, cut into thin julienne strips
1 celery stalk, cut into julienne strips
1 (2-inch) piece gingerroot, cut into julienne strips
1 tablespoon wine vinegar
1 tablespoon soy sauce
Salt
Freshly ground pepper

---

1. Preheat oven to 375F (190C). Grease a piece of foil large enough to completely enclose fish. Place fish on greased foil. Brush fish with honey; sprinkle with carrot, celery, gingerroot, wine vinegar and soy sauce. Season with salt and pepper.
2. Fold over foil to completely enclose fish; seal edges. Place on a baking sheet.
3. Bake in preheated oven 8 to 10 minutes per inch of thickness of fish, measured at the thickest part, or until fish tests done.
4. Remove from foil to serve. Pour any cooking juices over fish. Makes 2 servings.

Ocean Pie

1 lb. white fish, skinned, boned
1 cup milk
Salt
Freshly ground pepper
4 oz. shrimp, cooked, peeled, deveined
6 tablespoons butter or margarine
3 tablespoons all-purpose flour
1 tablespoon chopped fresh parsley
2 teaspoons grated lemon peel
4 cups chopped peeled potatoes (about 1-1/2 lb.)
1 cup shredded Cheddar cheese (4 oz.)

To garnish:
Lemon twists
Finely chopped fresh parsley

---

1. Preheat oven to 375F (190C). Place fish, milk, salt and pepper in a medium saucepan. Bring to a simmer. Cover and poach about 5 minutes or until fish tests done. Drain fish, reserving milk; flake fish into small pieces.
2. In a 1-1/2-quart casserole, combine flaked fish and shrimp.
3. Melt 3 tablespoons butter or margarine in a medium saucepan. Stir in flour; cook 1 minute, stirring. Gradually stir in reserved milk to make a smooth sauce. Boil 2 minutes, stirring. Stir in parsley and lemon peel; pour over fish mixture. Keep warm.
4. Meanwhile, cook potatoes in a pan of salted boiling water about 20 minutes or until tender. Drain and mash potatoes. Stir in remaining 3 tablespoons butter or margarine. Stir in 1/2 of cheese. Spoon potatoes around edge of fish mixture; sprinkle with remaining cheese.
5. Bake in preheated oven 20 to 25 minutes or until golden brown. Garnish with lemon twists and parsley. Makes 4 servings.

Do not overcook fish. It is already tender and cooks quickly. Cook only until firm and opaque. To test for doneness, cut into the center of the thickest part. It should be slightly opaque. One rule is to cook fresh or thawed fish 10 minutes per inch of thickness and to cook frozen fish 20 minutes per inch of thickness. However, this is only a general guide; cooking time will vary with the oven temperature and the shape and type of fish. Overcooked fish is tough and dry.

Left to right: Honey-Baked Fish, Ocean Pie

Mushrooms & Ham with toast, Bacon-Stuffed Potato

Mushrooms & Ham

1/2 cup butter or margarine, room temperature
8 oz. button mushrooms
2 cups finely chopped cooked ham (about 8 oz.)
1/4 cup Madeira
1/4 cup whipping cream
1 cup shredded sharp Cheddar cheese (4 oz.)
1 teaspoon Italian seasoning
4 white-bread slices, crusts removed
Paprika

To garnish:
Parsley sprigs

This dish is a specialty of an award-winning restaurant near Amersham in Buckinghamshire, England. The secret of its success lies in choosing the smallest mushrooms available and using a rich Madeira.

1. Preheat broiler. Melt 1/4 cup butter or margarine in a medium saucepan. Add mushrooms; sauté about 4 minutes or until softened. Add ham; cook 2 minutes.
2. Stir in Madeira; boil 1 minute to reduce slightly. Stir in cream; simmer 2 minutes.
3. Spoon mixture into a large shallow flameproof dish or 4 individual flameproof dishes; sprinkle with cheese.
4. Broil under preheated broiler until bubbly. Sprinkle with paprika; garnish with parsley. Keep hot.
5. In a small bowl, blend remaining 1/4 cup butter or margarine and Italian seasoning. Spread herb mixture on both sides of bread. Place herbed bread on a baking sheet. Toast bread under preheated broiler on both sides until golden. Cut each slice in half lengthwise; serve with hot mushroom mixture. Makes 4 servings.

Bacon-Stuffed Potatoes

4 large baking potatoes
8 bacon slices, chopped
4 oz. mushrooms, sliced (about 1-3/4 cups)
1/2 cup dairy sour cream
Salt
Freshly ground pepper
2 tablespoons chopped fresh chives

To garnish:
4 bacon slices

1. Preheat oven to 375F (190C). Prick potatoes. Place pricked potatoes on a baking sheet.
2. Bake potatoes in preheated oven 1 hour or until tender.
3. Meanwhile, in a medium skillet, cook bacon with no added fat until crisp and golden. Drain off all but 2 tablespoons fat. Add mushrooms to bacon; cook 5 minutes.
4. Slice off tops of baked potatoes; scoop out potatoes into a medium bowl, reserving potato skins. Stir mushroom mixture, 1/4 cup sour cream, salt and pepper into potatoes. Fold in 1 tablespoon chives. Spoon mixture into reserved potato skins. Place stuffed potatoes on a baking sheet.
5. Bake 10 minutes. Keep warm.
6. Preheat broiler. To make bacon garnishes, pleat bacon onto a skewer. Broil under preheated broiler until golden.
7. Spoon remaining sour cream over baked stuffed potatoes. Top each potato with a broiled bacon slice and remaining chives. Makes 4 servings.

One-Dish Meals

Nasi Goreng

1-1/4 cups uncooked long-grain white rice
Salt
1/4 cup butter or margarine
1 lb. lean pork, cut into 1/4-inch-wide strips
2 onions, sliced
1 red bell pepper, chopped
1/2 cup green peas
1/4 cucumber, chopped
1 carrot, shredded
1/4 cup soy sauce
1 teaspoon curry powder
Pinch of five-spice powder
Freshly ground black pepper

Omelet:
1 egg
1 teaspoon cold water
Salt
Freshly ground black pepper
1 tablespoon butter or margarine

To garnish:
2 tomatoes, cut into wedges
Green-onion curls, page 58

Nasi Goreng is an Indonesian dish. If kept warm and covered, it can stand up to 30 minutes before serving.

1. In a medium saucepan, cook rice in boiling salted water according to package directions. Rice should be tender and water absorbed. Set aside.
2. Melt butter or margarine in a large skillet. Add pork; cook 5 to 8 minutes or until golden. Add onions; cook 10 minutes.
3. Add bell pepper, peas, cucumber and carrot to pork mixture; cook 5 minutes. Stir in soy sauce, curry powder, five-spice powder, salt and black pepper. Stir in cooked rice until combined and hot.
4. To make omelet, in a small bowl, beat egg with water, salt and pepper. Melt butter or margarine in a small skillet; add egg mixture. Cook gently until underside is golden. Turn and brown other side. Slide onto a plate; cut into 1/2-inch-wide strips.
5. Spoon rice mixture into a warmed serving dish; top with a lattice of omelet strips. Garnish with tomato wedges and green-onion curls. Makes 4 to 6 servings.

French Onion Soup with Cheese Toast

1/4 cup butter or margarine
1 tablespoon vegetable oil
4 medium onions, thinly sliced
1/2 teaspoon sugar
2 tablespoons all-purpose flour
3-1/2 cups beef stock
Salt
Freshly ground pepper
4 thick bread slices
1 garlic clove, halved
1 cup shredded Gruyére cheese (4 oz.)
2 tablespoons brandy, if desired

1. Heat butter or margarine and oil in a large heavy saucepan. Add onions; cover. Cook over medium heat 20 minutes, stirring occasionally.
2. Stir in sugar. Cook, uncovered, until onions turn golden, stirring frequently.
3. Stir in flour; cook 1 minute. Gradually stir in stock. Season with salt and pepper. Bring to a boil; reduce heat. Simmer 20 minutes.
4. Preheat broiler. Rub bread slices with cut-side of garlic. Place seasoned bread on a baking sheet. Toast under preheated broiler. Turn over; sprinkle with cheese. Broil until golden and bubbly. Cut bread slices into thick strips.
5. Stir brandy into soup, if desired. Ladle hot soup into warmed soup bowls. Add toasted bread strips; serve immediately. Makes 4 servings.

Left to right: French Onion Soup with Cheese Toast, Nasi Goreng

Chunky Gazpacho

2 bread slices, crusts removed
2 cups tomato juice
2 garlic cloves, crushed
1/2 cucumber, peeled, finely chopped
1 green bell pepper, chopped
1 red bell pepper, chopped
1 large onion, finely chopped
4 to 6 medium tomatoes, peeled, seeded,
    chopped (1-1/2 lb.)
1/4 cup olive oil
2 tablespoons red-wine vinegar
Salt
Freshly ground black pepper
1/4 teaspoon dried leaf marjoram
1/4 teaspoon dried leaf basil
Fresh cilantro sprig

To serve:
Croutons
Sliced pimento-stuffed olives
Coarsely chopped cucumber
Chopped green and red bell peppers
Chopped green onions

A classic Spanish soup, Gazpacho makes a refreshing light supper or lunch dish. Guests sprinkle their bowls of soup with a little of each garnish before eating.

1. Chop bread coarsely. Place chopped bread, tomato juice and garlic in a blender. Let stand 5 minutes; blend until smooth. Or, place bread, tomato juice and garlic in a medium bowl. Mash with a wooden spoon until blended.
2. In a medium bowl, combine bread mixture, cucumber, bell peppers, onion, tomatoes, olive oil, vinegar, salt, black pepper, marjoram and basil. Transfer to a chilled soup tureen or serving dish.
3. Refrigerate 1 hour or until chilled. Garnish with cilantro sprig. Serve with small bowls of croutons, olives, cucumber, bell peppers and green onions. Accompany with crusty French bread. Makes 4 servings.

> To make *flavored croutons,* deep-fry bread cubes in hot oil until crisp and golden. Drain fried croutons on paper towels. Toss in coarse sea salt, freshly grated lemon peel, finely chopped fresh herbs, garlic salt, onion salt, finely grated Parmesan cheese or lemon pepper for delicious results.

Hearty Minestrone

8 bacon slices, diced
2 garlic cloves, crushed
4 celery stalks, chopped
4 carrots, sliced
2 onions, chopped
2 potatoes, peeled, diced (about 12 oz.)
1 (1-lb.) can tomatoes
1 cup chicken stock
1 parsley sprig
1 bay leaf
1 tablespoon chopped fresh basil
Salt
Freshly ground pepper
1 (15-oz.) can white beans or garbanzo beans, drained
2 oz. spaghetti
8 oz. ham, cut into thin strips
1/2 small head cabbage, shredded
2 zucchini, sliced
1/2 (10-oz.) pkg. frozen green beans

To garnish:
4 to 6 tablespoons grated Parmesan cheese
4 to 6 fresh basil sprigs, if desired

1. Place bacon in a large flameproof casserole; cook until crisp. Drain off all but 2 tablespoons fat. Add garlic, celery, carrots, onions and potatoes; cook 5 minutes, stirring frequently.
2. Add tomatoes with their juice, stock, parsley, bay leaf, basil, salt and pepper. Cover and simmer 20 minutes.
3. Add canned beans; spaghetti, broken into small pieces; ham; cabbage; zucchini and green beans. Cover and cook 10 minutes or until spaghetti is tender.
4. Remove and discard parsley and bay leaf. Ladle soup into a warmed soup tureen or soup bowls.
5. Sprinkle with Parmesan cheese; garnish with a few basil sprigs, if desired. Makes 4 to 6 servings.

Provence-Style Fish Chowder

3 tablespoons vegetable oil
3 large onions, finely chopped
1 garlic clove, crushed
1 (28-oz.) can tomatoes
1 parsley sprig
1 bay leaf
3 cups chopped peeled potatoes (about 1 lb.)
About 20 small black olives, pitted
2 tablespoons capers
1 cup tomato juice
2 cups chicken, vegetable or fish stock
Salt
Freshly ground pepper
1-1/2 lb. white fish, skinned, boned, cut into
    3/4-inch cubes

To garnish:
3 tablespoons finely chopped fresh parsley

1. Heat oil in a large saucepan. Add onions and garlic; sauté over low heat about 5 minutes or until lightly browned.
2. Add tomatoes with their juice, parsley and bay leaf. Bring to a boil. Reduce heat; simmer 5 minutes, stirring frequently to break up tomatoes.
3. Add potatoes, olives, capers, tomato juice, stock, salt and pepper. Cook, uncovered, 10 to 15 minutes or until potatoes are almost tender.
4. Stir in fish; simmer over low heat, uncovered, about 5 minutes or until fish tests done.
5. Remove and discard parsley sprig and bay leaf. Transfer to a warmed serving dish or tureen. Garnish with parsley. Serve hot with thick wedges of crusty bread. Makes 4 to 6 servings.

Clockwise from left: Chunky Gazpacho with accompaniments, Hearty Minestrone, Provence-Style Fish Chowder

Lattice-Topped Meat Pie

Meat Filling:
2 tablespoons vegetable oil
2 bacon slices, diced
1 onion, chopped
1 garlic clove, crushed, if desired
1 celery stalk, chopped
1 large carrot, chopped
1 lb. lean ground beef
1 (8-oz.) can tomatoes, chopped
1/4 cup dry red wine or beef stock
Salt
Freshly ground pepper
Pinch of freshly grated nutmeg

Lattice Topping:
2-1/4 cups chopped, peeled potatoes (about 12 oz.)
1 large rutabaga or 3 parsnips, peeled
3 tablespoons butter or margarine
1/4 cup half and half or milk
1/4 cup shredded Cheddar cheese (1 oz.)
Salt
White pepper

To garnish:
Tomato slices
1 parsley sprig

1. To make filling, heat oil in a large saucepan. Add bacon, onion, garlic, celery and carrot; sauté over medium heat 5 minutes.
2. Stir in beef; cook about 10 minutes or until lightly browned. Drain off excess fat.
3. Stir in tomatoes, wine or stock, salt, pepper and nutmeg. Simmer over low heat about 15 minutes or until thickened. Spoon into an ovenproof dish.
4. To make topping, in a large saucepan, cook potatoes and rutabaga or parsnips in boiling salted water about 20 minutes or until tender.
5. Preheat oven to 425F (220C). Drain and mash cooked potatoes and rutabaga or parsnips. Beat in butter or margarine, half and half or milk, cheese, salt and white pepper until smooth. Spoon into a pastry bag fitted with a large star-shaped tip. Pipe a lattice over top of meat filling.
6. Bake in preheated oven 20 minutes or until lattice is golden and crisp. Garnish with tomato slices and parsley sprig. Makes 4 servings.

Ham & Potato Gratin

1-1/2 cups thinly sliced peeled potatoes (8 oz.)
8 oz. sliced ham
2 onions, sliced
1-1/2 cups shredded Cheddar cheese (6 oz.)
Salt
Freshly ground pepper
1 teaspoon freshly grated nutmeg
2 eggs
1 cup milk
3 tablespoons whipping cream
2 tablespoons butter or margarine

To garnish:
Parsley sprigs or celery leaves

1. Preheat oven to 325F (165C). Grease a 1-1/2-quart casserole. Place alternate layers of potato, ham, onion and cheese in greased casserole, ending with ham. Season each layer with salt, pepper and nutmeg.
2. In a medium bowl, beat eggs, milk and cream until blended; pour over ham. Dot with butter or margarine.
3. Bake in preheated oven 1-1/2 hours or until potatoes are tender and topping is golden brown.
4. Garnish with parsley sprigs or celery leaves. Serve from baking dish. Serve with a vegetable salad. Makes 4 to 6 servings.

Variations
Tongue & Potato Gratin: Substitute 8 ounces sliced cooked tongue for ham.
Bacon & Potato Gratin: Substitute 8 slices crumbled crisp-cooked bacon for ham.

Top to bottom: Lattice-Topped Meat Pie, Ham & Potato Gratin

Spicy Moroccan Chicken

1/4 cup honey
1 teaspoon curry powder
1/2 teaspoon freshly ground pepper
1 teaspoon salt
Pinch of ground allspice
1 (3-1/4-lb.) roasting chicken, cut into serving pieces
1 lemon, thinly sliced
1 cup water
1/4 cup butter or margarine
1 cup chicken stock
1/4 cup raisins
Chopped fresh parsley

1. In a small bowl, combine 2 tablespoons honey, curry powder, pepper, salt and allspice. Spread over chicken pieces; place coated chicken in a glass or stainless-steel bowl. Cover and refrigerate overnight.
2. Drain any liquid from chicken into a medium saucepan. Add lemon slices and water; cook 10 minutes over low heat.
3. Melt butter or margarine and remaining 2 tablespoons honey in a large flameproof casserole. Add marinated chicken pieces; cook about 15 to 20 minutes or until chicken is a deep golden brown on all sides.
4. Add hot lemon mixture, stock and raisins to casserole. Bring to a boil; reduce heat. Cover and simmer 30 to 35 minutes or until chicken is tender.
5. Sprinkle with chopped parsley; serve hot with warm pita bread. Makes 4 servings.

Chicken Stew with Bacon Dumplings

2 to 3 tablespoons vegetable oil
1 (3-1/2- to 4-lb.) roasting chicken, cut into serving pieces
1 large garlic clove, crushed
12 to 16 small white onions
2 tablespoons all-purpose flour
2-1/2 cups chicken stock
1 bay leaf
1-1/2 teaspoons Italian seasoning
Salt
Freshly ground pepper
8 oz. small mushrooms, trimmed

Bacon Dumplings:
1 cup all-purpose flour
1 teaspoon baking powder
1/2 teaspoon Italian seasoning
1/2 teaspoon salt
1 small onion, finely chopped
4 bacon slices, crisp-cooked, crumbled
2 tablespoons vegetable oil
1/2 cup milk

To garnish:
Freshly chopped parsley

1. Heat oil in a Dutch oven. Add chicken pieces; cook until browned on all sides. Remove chicken with tongs; set aside.
2. Add garlic and onions to fat remaining in pan; sauté until onions are golden. Remove onions with slotted spoon; set aside.
3. Stir flour into pan drippings; cook 1 minute, stirring. Gradually stir in stock; cook, stirring constantly, until mixture thickens and comes to a boil. Stir in bay leaf, Italian seasoning, salt and pepper. Return chicken and onions to pan. Cover and cook over low heat 30 to 35 minutes or until chicken is tender.
4. To make dumplings, in a medium bowl, combine flour, baking powder, Italian seasoning and salt. Stir in onion and bacon. In a small bowl, combine oil and milk; stir into flour mixture until blended.
5. Remove and discard bay leaf from stew. Stir in mushrooms. Drop dumplings by tablespoonfuls onto hot stew. Lower heat; simmer, uncovered, 10 minutes. Cover and simmer 10 to 12 minutes or until dumplings are cooked. Sprinkle with parsley; serve from pan. Makes 4 servings.

Variation
Parsley & Lemon Dumplings: Substitute 1-1/2 tablespoons freshly chopped parsley, 1 teaspoon grated lemon peel and 1 tablespoon lemon juice for Italian seasoning and bacon.

Chicken Catalan

6 tablespoon olive oil
6 chicken-breast halves, with wings attached, if desired
3 onions, sliced
2 garlic cloves, crushed
2-1/2 cups uncooked long-grain white rice
2 tablespoons tomato paste
3/4 teaspoon ground turmeric
5 cups hot chicken stock
1 teaspoon paprika
Salt
Freshly ground black pepper
4 oz. cooked Italian sausage, skinned, cut into bite-sized pieces
1 green bell pepper, sliced
1 red bell pepper, sliced
1/2 cup pimento-stuffed olives
1 tablespoon chopped fresh parsley

1. Heat 3 tablespoons oil in a large flameproof casserole. Add chicken; cook about 15 minutes or until lightly browned on both sides. Remove with a slotted spoon; keep warm.
2. Add onions and garlic to pan juices; cook 2 to 3 minutes or until softened.
3. Add remaining oil and rice to casserole; cook until rice turns a light golden color, stirring.
4. Stir in tomato paste, turmeric, stock, paprika, salt and black pepper. Bring to a boil; add browned chicken, sausage and bell peppers, pressing them into rice mixture. Reduce heat; simmer, covered, about 30 minutes or until rice is tender, stirring occasionally.
5. Stir in olives; cook 2 to 3 minutes to warm through. Sprinkle with parsley; serve from casserole. Makes 6 servings.

Left to right: Chicken Stew with Bacon Dumplings, Chicken Catalan

Chicken & Sausage Pot Pies

3/4 lb. bulk Italian sausage
1/2 teaspoon rubbed sage or Italian seasoning
1 tablespoon prepared mustard
2 tablespoons butter or margarine
1 lb. chicken cutlets, trimmed, cut into cubes
8 oz. mushrooms, sliced (about 3-1/4 cups)
1 large onion, chopped
1 garlic clove, crushed
2 tablespoons all-purpose flour
1 cup chicken stock
1/2 cup dry white wine or dry sherry
Salt
Freshly ground pepper

Biscuit Topping:
1-1/2 cups all-purpose flour
2 teaspoons baking powder
1/2 teaspoon Italian seasoning
1/4 teaspoon salt
1/4 cup butter or margarine
7 tablespoons milk
1 egg yolk beaten with 1 tablespoon milk for glaze

1. In a medium bowl, combine sausage, sage or Italian seasoning and mustard. Shape mixture into 12 (1-1/2-inch) balls; set aside.
2. Melt butter or margarine in a large skillet. Add chicken; cook over medium heat until lightly browned. Remove chicken with a slotted spoon; set aside. Add sausage balls to skillet; cook until browned on all sides. Remove with a slotted spoon; set aside. Drain off all but 2 tablespoons fat from skillet.
3. Add mushrooms, onion and garlic to skillet; sauté until onion is transparent. Sprinkle flour over mushroom mixture; cook 1 minute, stirring. Gradually stir in stock and wine or sherry; cook, stirring, until sauce is thickened and comes to a boil. Return chicken and sausage to skillet. Season with salt and pepper. Simmer 5 minutes, stirring occasionally.
4. Preheat oven to 425F (220C). To make Biscuit Topping, in a medium bowl, combine flour, baking powder, Italian seasoning and salt. With a pastry blender or 2 knives, cut in butter or margarine until mixture resembles coarse crumbs. Stir in milk to make a soft dough. Knead in bowl 8 to 10 strokes.
5. On a lightly floured surface, roll out dough to about 1/2 inch thick. Cut with a floured 2-inch round cutter.
6. Spoon chicken-sausage mixture into 4 (1-3/4- to 2-cup) casseroles. Arrange biscuits, slightly overlapping, on top. Brush biscuit tops with egg glaze.
7. Bake 20 to 25 minutes or until biscuits are golden brown. Makes 4 servings.

Variation
Sesame Topping: Make topping as above. Glaze and sprinkle with sesame seeds. Bake as above.

Liver & Bacon with Wine Sauce

4 bacon slices, halved
1/4 cup all-purpose flour
Salt
Freshly ground pepper
1 lb. calves' liver, thinly sliced
1/4 cup dry red wine
1/2 cup beef stock
1/4 cup lemon juice
2 teaspoons cornstarch, if desired
Water, if desired

To garnish:
Chopped fresh parsley
Lemon twists

1. In a large heavy skillet, sauté bacon with no added fat until crisp. Remove with a slotted spoon; drain on paper towels.
2. In a shallow bowl, combine flour, salt and pepper. Coat liver with seasoned flour. Add coated liver to skillet; cook about 5 minutes or until browned on both sides. Gradually stir in wine, stock and lemon juice. Cover and simmer 10 to 15 minutes or until liver is tender.
3. If desired, in a small bowl, blend cornstarch with a little water. Stir cornstarch mixture into cooking liquid. Cook until thickened, stirring.
4. Garnish with chopped parsley and lemon twists. Top with drained bacon. Serve hot with cooked carrots or other vegetables. Makes 4 servings.

Top to bottom: Chicken & Sausage Pot Pies, Liver & Bacon with Wine Sauce

Pork & Mango Curry

3 tablespoons all-purpose flour
1-1/2 lb. pork tenderloin, cut into 1-inch cubes
2 tablespoons vegetable oil
1 onion, thickly sliced
2 small green or red bell peppers, sliced
1 teaspoon ground turmeric
1 teaspoon salt
1 tablespoon curry powder
1 teaspoon ground cumin
1 teaspoon ground ginger
1/2 teaspoon ground chilies
5 medium tomatoes, peeled, seeded, chopped
2 teaspoons tomato paste
1-1/2 cups chicken stock
1-1/2 lb. small new potatoes, scrubbed or peeled
    (about 8 to 12)
1 (15-oz.) can mango slices, drained, or
    2 large mangoes, peeled, stoned, sliced

1. Place flour in a plastic bag. Add pork cubes; toss to coat. Heat oil in a large flameproof casserole. Add coated pork; sauté about 5 minutes or until golden. Add onion and bell peppers; cook 3 minutes.
2. Stir in turmeric, salt, curry powder, cumin, ginger and ground chilies. Cook 1 minute, stirring constantly.
3. Stir in tomatoes, tomato paste and stock. Add potatoes; cover and cook 15 minutes over low heat, stirring occasionally. Add mango slices; cook 5 minutes or until potatoes are tender.
4. Serve curry with a selection of accompaniments, such as hot cooked rice, sliced bananas dipped in lemon juice, shredded coconut, mango chutney, poppadums, chopped cucumber in plain yogurt, or a crisp green salad. For information about poppadums, see comments in recipe for Tropical Curried-Chicken Salad, page 38. Makes 4 to 6 servings.

Stir-Fried Beef & Vegetables

12 oz. beef round steak
1/4 cup vegetable oil
3 carrots, cut into julienne strips
1 red or yellow bell pepper, sliced
1 bunch green onions, sliced into 1-inch lengths
1 (10-oz.) can miniature corn-on-the-cob, drained
1 garlic clove, crushed
1 teaspoon cornstarch
6 tablespoons red wine or apple cider
2 tablespoons soy sauce
1/2 cup beef stock
Salt
Freshly ground black pepper
1/2 (10-oz.) pkg. frozen green peas, thawed
4 oz. bean sprouts (1 cup)

To serve:
Cooked green noodles or white rice

To garnish:
1 green onion cut into julienne strips.

1. Slice beef into thin strips across grain. Heat 2 tablespoons oil in a large skillet or wok over high heat. Add beef strips; stir-fry 2 to 3 minutes. Remove cooked beef with a slotted spoon; keep warm.
2. Add remaining oil to skillet or wok; heat until hot. When hot, add carrots, bell pepper, green onions, corn and garlic. Stir-fry over high heat 3 to 4 minutes.
3. In a small bowl, blend cornstarch and wine or cider. Stir cornstarch mixture, soy sauce and stock into vegetable mixture. Bring to a boil, stirring constantly. Season with salt and black pepper.
4. Add cooked beef, peas and bean sprouts; cook 2 minutes to heat through.
5. Arrange green noodles or rice on a serving plate. Spoon beef mixture over noodles or rice. Garnish with green onion. Makes 4 servings.

Left to right: Pork & Mango Curry with accompaniments,
Eggplant Moussaka, Stir-Fried Beef & Vegetables

Eggplant Moussaka

6 tablespoons vegetable oil
1 onion, chopped
12 oz. lean ground beef
2 teaspoons tomato paste
1 (8-oz.) can tomato sauce
Salt
Freshly ground pepper
2 medium eggplants, thinly sliced
8 oz. plain yogurt (1 cup)
2 eggs, beaten
3 tablespoons grated Parmesan cheese

1. Preheat oven to 375F (190C). Grease a 2-quart casserole. Heat 2 tablespoons oil in a medium saucepan. Add onion; cook about 5 minutes or until softened.
2. Add beef; cook about 5 minutes or until lightly browned, stirring to break up beef. Drain off excess fat. Stir in tomato paste and tomato sauce. Season with salt and pepper. Simmer over a low heat 5 minutes.
3. Meanwhile, heat remaining oil in a large skillet. Add eggplant slices; cook until lightly browned. Drain on paper towels.
4. Place alternate layers of beef mixture and cooked eggplant slices in greased casserole, beginning and ending with eggplant slices.
5. In a small bowl, beat yogurt, eggs, salt and pepper. Spoon over moussaka; sprinkle with Parmesan cheese.
6. Bake in preheated oven 30 minutes or until top is golden and mixture is bubbly. Serve hot with a tossed salad and French bread. Makes 4 servings.

Potato-Topped Pork Bake

2 tablespoons vegetable oil
1 onion, sliced
1 lb. pork tenderloin, cut into 1-inch cubes
1 (1-lb.) can tomatoes
4 small leeks, white parts only, sliced
4 small zucchini, sliced
1 teaspoon finely chopped fresh basil
Salt
Freshly ground pepper
3 cups thinly sliced peeled potatoes (1 lb.)
1 cup shredded Cheddar cheese (4 oz.)

To garnish:
Parsley sprigs

1. Preheat oven to 350 (175C). Heat oil in a 2-quart flame-proof casserole. Add onion and pork; cook, stirring, about 10 minutes or until browned.
2. Stir in tomatoes with their juice, leeks, zucchini, basil, salt and pepper. Remove from heat; layer potatoes over meat mixture. Cover casserole.
3. Bake in preheated oven 30 minutes. Sprinkle potatoes with cheese; bake, uncovered, 20 minutes or until potatoes are tender and cheese is melted. Garnish with parsley sprigs. Makes 4 servings.

Left to right: Potato-Topped Pork Bake, Sweet & Sour Pork Balls with Bean-Sprout Salad

Sweet & Sour Pork Balls

1-1/4 lb. lean ground pork
1 cup fresh bread crumbs
1/2 small onion, finely chopped
1/2 teaspoon rubbed sage
1 large egg yolk, beaten
Salt
Freshly ground pepper
2 tablespoons vegetable oil

Sweet & Sour Sauce:
1 (1-lb.) can apricot halves in light syrup
2 tablespoons cornstarch
1/4 cup soy sauce
1/4 cup ketchup
1/2 cup chicken stock
1 small green bell pepper, chopped
1 small red bell pepper, chopped
1 tablespoon chopped gingerroot

---

1. In a medium bowl, combine pork, bread crumbs, onion, sage, egg yolk, salt and pepper. Shape into 24 small balls.
2. Heat oil in a large heavy skillet. Add pork balls; sauté over medium heat about 15 minutes or until browned, turning occasionally. Remove with a slotted spoon; drain on paper towels. Keep warm.
3. To make sauce, drain apricots, reserving syrup. In a medium saucepan, combine cornstarch and reserved syrup. Stir in soy sauce, ketchup and stock. Bring to a boil, stirring constantly.
4. Reduce heat; stir in bell peppers and gingerroot; simmer 5 minutes.
5. Add pork balls, coating with sauce; simmer about 5 minutes, stirring frequently.
6. Slice apricots; gently stir into pork mixture. Serve immediately with cooked rice and Bean-Sprout Salad; see box. Makes 4 servings.

Bean-Sprout Salad: In a medium salad bowl, combine 1-1/2 cups bean sprouts and 2 cups sliced mushrooms. To make dressing, in a small bowl, whisk together 3 tablespoons olive oil, 1/4 cup fresh orange juice, 1 tablespoon lemon peel, salt and freshly ground pepper. Pour dressing over salad; toss to combine.

Chili con Carne

3 tablespoons vegetable oil
2 onions, chopped
1 garlic clove, crushed
1 lb. lean ground beef
2 teaspoons dried leaf oregano
1 teaspoon ground cumin
2 teaspoons chili powder
1 teaspoon paprika
Salt
Freshly ground pepper
1 (1-lb.) can tomatoes
1/2 cup beef stock
6 oz. chorizo sausage, skinned, coarsely chopped
1 (15-oz.) can red kidney beans, drained

This is a speedy but extra-tasty version of classic chili con carne. It has a hot spicy taste that comes not only from the chili powder but also from chorizo sausage. Mexican chorizo sausage can be bought at most good delicatessens and is easily recognizable by its bright red color. It is pork sausage flavored with hot red pepper. If it is difficult to find, use any cured sausage with a hot spicy flavor. Flavor of chili improves when it is made a day ahead and reheated.

1. Heat oil in a large saucepan. Add onions and garlic; cook 5 to 10 minutes or until softened.
2. Add beef; cook about 10 minutes or until lightly browned, stirring to break up beef. Stir in oregano, cumin, chili powder, paprika, salt and pepper. Cook over medium heat 2 to 3 minutes.
3. Coarsely chop tomatoes; stir chopped tomatoes and their juice into beef mixture. Stir in stock. Cook, uncovered, over medium heat 10 to 15 minutes.
4. Stir in chorizo sausage and beans; cook 10 minutes.
5. Serve hot with cooked rice or warm tortillas. Makes 4 servings.

Beef Carbonnade

1 tablespoon butter or margarine
4 bacon slices, diced
3 large onions, sliced
1 garlic clove, crushed
2 lb. beef for stew, cut into 1-inch cubes
2 tablespoons all-purpose flour
1 teaspoon brown sugar
1 tablespoon red-wine vinegar
2 cups ale or dark beer
1 bay leaf
1 parsley sprig
1 (2-inch) piece orange peel
Salt
Freshly ground pepper
Freshly grated nutmeg
8 oz. small mushrooms

To garnish:
Orange peel

---

1. Preheat oven to 300F (150C). Melt butter or margarine in a large flameproof casserole. Add bacon; cook until crisp. Remove with a slotted spoon; drain on paper towels.
2. Add onions and garlic to casserole. Cook over medium heat until softened. Remove with a slotted spoon; set aside.
3. Add beef to casserole; brown on all sides, stirring occasionally. Remove with a slotted spoon; keep warm.
4. Stir flour into fat remaining in casserole; cook 1 minute. Stir in sugar and vinegar; cook until dark brown. Gradually stir in ale or beer.
5. Stir in cooked bacon, onion mixture, browned beef, bay leaf, parsley, orange peel, salt, pepper and nutmeg to taste. Cover casserole with a lid or foil.
6. Cook in preheated oven 2 hours or until beef is tender. Remove and discard bay leaf, parsley sprig and orange peel. Stir in mushrooms. Cover and cook 10 to 15 minutes. Serve hot with boiled potatoes or cooked rice. Makes 6 servings.

Lamb Navarin with Herbed Choux Buns

3 tablespoons vegetable oil
8 to 10 small white onions
2 lb. lamb for stew, cut into 1-inch cubes
2 garlic cloves, crushed
3 tablespoons all-purpose flour
2-1/2 cups chicken broth
1/4 cup tomato paste
1 teaspoon paprika
1/2 teaspoon dried leaf thyme
1/2 teaspoon dried leaf marjoram
Salt
Freshly ground pepper
9 to 12 small new potatoes, peeled
4 small white turnips, quartered
1 (12-oz.) pkg. baby carrots
1/2 (10-oz.) pkg. frozen green peas

Herbed Choux Buns:
1/2 cup water
1/4 cup butter or margarine
1/4 teaspoon salt
1/2 cup all-purpose flour
2 eggs
1/4 cup shredded sharp Cheddar cheese (1 oz.)
1/2 teaspoon Italian seasoning

---

1. Heat oil in a 2-1/2- to 3-quart flameproof casserole. Add onions; sauté until golden. Remove onions with a slotted spoon; set aside. Add lamb to casserole; cook until browned on all sides. Remove lamb with a slotted spoon; set aside.
2. Add garlic to casserole; cook 1 minute. Stir in flour; cook 1 minute, stirring. Gradually stir in broth; cook, stirring constantly, until mixture is thickened and comes to a boil. Stir in tomato paste, paprika, thyme, marjoram, salt and pepper. Return lamb and onions to casserole. Stir in potatoes, turnips and carrots. Cover and cook over low heat 30 to 40 minutes or until lamb and vegetables are almost tender, stirring occasionally. Stir peas into casserole.
3. Preheat oven to 425F (220C). To make Herbed Choux Buns, bring water, butter or margarine and salt to a boil in a medium saucepan. Add flour, all at once. With a wooden spoon, beat until dough forms a ball that leaves side of pan. Remove from heat; cool slightly. Beat in eggs, 1 at a time, beating well after each addition.
4. Stir in cheese and Italian seasoning until blended. Spoon choux mixture in small mounds around edge of hot casserole.
5. Bake in preheated oven 20 to 25 minutes or until choux buns are puffed and golden brown. Makes 6 servings.

Left to right: Beef Carbonnade, Lamb Navarin with Herbed Choux Buns

Greek-Style Meatballs

3 bread slices, crusts removed
1/4 cup water
1-1/2 lb. lean ground lamb
1 onion, finely chopped
1 garlic clove, crushed
1 teaspoon finely chopped fresh thyme
Salt
Freshly ground pepper

Sauce:
3 egg yolks
3 to 4 tablespoons lemon juice
1/2 cup water
Salt
White pepper

To garnish:
Shredded crisp lettuce
Lemon slices

1. Soak bread in water 5 minutes; squeeze to remove excess water. In a medium bowl, combine soaked bread, lamb, onion, garlic, thyme, salt and pepper. With damp hands, form mixture into 25 to 30 (1-inch) balls.
2. Bring a large saucepan of salted water to a boil. Add meatballs; simmer over low heat about 20 minutes or until no longer pink inside. Drain on paper towels.
3. To make sauce, beat egg yolks in top of a double boiler over hot water until foamy. Beat in 3 tablespoons lemon juice, water, salt and white pepper. Cook, stirring constantly, over low heat until sauce has thickened slightly. Stir in additional lemon juice to taste.
4. Add meatballs to sauce, stirring to coat; heat through. Place lettuce on a serving plate; spoon meatballs and sauce over lettuce. Garnish with lemon slices. Serve with a tomato-and-onion salad. Makes 4 servings.

Index

A

Apple Kabobs, Beef, Apricot & 19
Apricot & Apple Kabobs, Beef, 19
Apricots & Cinnamon, Pork with 48
Asparagus & Cheese Sandwiches,
Broiled 17

B

Bacon Dumplings, Chicken Stew
with 70
Bacon-Stuffed Potatoes 63
Bacon with Wine Sauce, Liver & 72
Baked Eggs Mornay 26
Bean Bundles, Crispy Beef & 25
Bean-Sprout Salad 77
Beef
Beef, Apricot & Apple Kabobs 19
Beef Carbonnade 78
Beef Patties with Chasseur
Sauce 24
Bobotie 56
Chili con Carne 77
Crispy Beef & Bean Bundles 25
Eggplant Moussaka 75
Lattice-Topped Meat Pie 69
Pork, Beef & Chicken Saté 10
Spicy Beef Stir-Fry 24
Steaks with Green-Peppercorn
Sauce 52
Stir-Fried Beef & Vegetables 74
Stroganoff-Topped Toast 19
Blue-Cheese Dressing, Mushroom
Puffs with 55
Bobotie 56

C

Calves' Liver with Sage 59
Camembert Puffs 28
Chasseur Sauce, Beef Patties
with 24
Cheese & Walnut Croquettes with
Watercress Dip 28
Cheese Flan, Ham & Smoked- 46
Cheese Fondue, Dutch- 26
Cheese Loaf, Baked Ham & 13
Cheese Pasta, Herbed- 22
Cheese Rolls, Beef & 15
Cheese Sandwiches, Bacon & 16
Cheese Sandwiches, Broiled
Asparagus & 17
Cheese Sauce, Pasta with Creamy
Ham & 55
Cheesy Onion Ring 42
Chicken Salad, Tropical
Curried- 38
Chicken
Chicken & Ham Loaf 40
Chicken & Sausage Pot Pies 72
Chicken Catalan 71
Chicken Stew with Bacon
Dumplings 70
Creamy Chicken Loaf
en Croûte 42
Orange- & Honey-Glazed Game
Hens 48
Pineapple- & Honey-Glazed
Game Hens 48
Pork, Beef & Chicken Saté 10
Roast Chicken 52
Spicy Moroccan Chicken 70
Chili con Carne 77

Choux Buns, Lamb Navarin with
Herbed 78
Cottage-Cheese Pancakes 30
Crab Gratinée 21
Crabmeat Soufflé, Dilled 26
Crepes, Seafood 33
Croutons, tip 66
Curry, Pork & Mango 74

D

Deviled Spanish Pizza 27
Dilled Crabmeat Soufflé 26
Duck with Plum Sauce 53
Dutch-Cheese Fondue 26

E

Egg Puffs, Fish & 33
Egg Snacks, Bean & 13
Eggplant Moussaka 75
Eggs Mornay, Baked 26

F

Farmhouse Pâté 44
Fish
Fish & Egg Puffs 33
Fish Chowder, Provence-Style 67
Fish Paprika 22
Honey-Baked Fish 61
Marinated Fish Kabobs 21
Ocean Pie 61
Pickled-Herring Salad 28
Potato & Fish Bake 32
Smoked-Salmon Mousse 41
Sole & Lime Pinwheels 20
Trout with Tarragon 61
Tuna-Stuffed Tomatoes 22
Flan, Ham & Smoked-Cheese 46
Fondue, Dutch-Cheese 26
French-Bread Pizzas 16
French Bread, Stuffed 45
French Onion Soup with
Cheese Toast 64
From the Pantry 22-33

G

Gazpacho, Chunky 66
Ginger, Pork with Orange & 48
Gougère, Ham & Mushroom 55
Green-Peppercorn Sauce, Steaks
with 52

H

Ham & Cheese Loaf, Baked 13
Ham & Cheese Sauce, Pasta with
Creamy 55
Ham & Mushroom Gougère 55
Ham & Potato Gratin 69
Ham & Smoked-Cheese Flan 46
Ham Loaf, Chicken & 40
Ham, Mushrooms & 62
Ham Quiche, Spanish
Vegetable & 47
Ham Salad, Cucumber, Melon & 36
Herbed-Cheese Pasta 22
Herring Salad, Pickled- 28
Honey-Glazed Game Hens,
Orange- & 48

I

Indonesian Lamb Kabobs 19
Introduction 6-9
Italian Platter 34

J

Japanese-Style Kidneys 58

K

Kabobs, Tropical 30
Kidneys, Japanese-Style 58

L

Lamb
Greek-Style Meatballs 79
Indonesian Lamb Kabobs 19
Lamb Navarin with Herbed
Choux Buns 78
Spicy Lamb en Papillote 51
Lime Pinwheels, Sole & 20
Liver & Bacon with Wine Sauce 72
Liver with Sage, Calves' 59

M

Mango Curry, Pork & 74
Meatballs, Greek-Style 79
Melon & Ham Salad, Cucumber, 36
Minestrone, Hearty 66
Mornay, Baked Eggs 26
Moussaka, Eggplant 75
Mousse, Smoked-Salmon 41
Mozzarella Snacks, Salami & 12
Mushroom Gougère, Ham & 55
Mushroom Puffs with Blue-Cheese
Dressing 55
Mushroom Quiche 45
Mushrooms & Ham 62
Mustard Sauce, Pork Chops with
Spicy 50

N

Nasi Goreng 64

O

Omelet, Spanish-Style 28
One-Dish Meals 64-79
Onion Ring, Cheesy 42
Onions, Stuffed 31
Orange & Ginger, Pork with 48
Orange Salad, Smoked-Trout & 37

P

Pancakes, Cottage-Cheese 30
Papaya, Ham-Stuffed 34
Papaya, tip 34
Pasta, Herbed-Cheese 22
Pasta, Seafood 38
Pasta with Creamy Ham & Cheese
Sauce 55
Pâté, Farmhouse 44
Pita-Pocket Sandwiches, Greek 10
Pizza, Deviled Spanish 27
Pizzas, French-Bread 16
Plum Sauce, Duck with 53
Pork
Pork & Mango Curry 74
Pork, Beef & Chicken Saté 10
Pork Chops with Spicy Mustard
Sauce 50
Pork with Apricots &
Cinnamon 48
Pork with Orange & Ginger 48
Potato-Topped Pork Bake 76
Sweet & Sour Pork Balls 77
Pot Pies, Chicken & Sausage 72
Potato & Fish Bake 32
Potato Gratin, Ham & 69
Potato-Topped Pork Bake 76
Potatoes, Bacon-Stuffed 63

Q

Quiche Lorraine 47
Quiche, Mushroom 45
Quiche, Spanish Vegetable &
Ham 47

S

Salads
Cucumber, Melon & Ham
Salad 36

Ham-Stuffed Papaya 34
Midsummer Chicken 37
Pear Waldorf Salad 40
Pickled-Herring Salad
Seafood Pasta 38
Smoked-Trout & Orange
Salad 37
Spicy Mexican Salad 38
Tropical Curried-Chicken
Salad 38
Salads, Pastries & Pâtés 34-47
**Sandwiches & Broiled
Dishes 10-21**
Sandwiches
Bacon & Cheese Sandwiches 16
Baked Ham & Cheese Loaf 13
Bean & Egg Snacks 13
Beef & Cheese Rolls 15
Broiled Asparagus & Cheese
Sandwiches 17
Greek Pita-Pocket
Sandwiches 10
New Yorkers 14
Salami & Mozzarella Snacks 12
Smorrebrod 14
Spicy Club Sandwiches 14
Stuffed French Bread 45
West Indies Pita-Pocket
Sandwiches 10
Sausage Pot Pies, Chicken & 72
Sausage Tarts 58
Seafood Crepes 33
Smorrebrod 14
Soufflé Surprises 57
Soufflé, Dilled Crabmeat 26
Soups
Chunky Gazpacho 66
French Onion Soup with
Cheese Toast 64
Hearty Minestrone 66
Provence-Style Fish Chowder 67
Spanish-Style Omelet 28
Spanish Vegetable & Ham
Quiche 47
Special Suppers 48-63
Stir-Fried Beef & Vegetables 74
Stir-Fry, Spicy Beef 24
Stroganoff-Topped Toast 19
Stuffed Onions 31

T

Tarts, Sausage 58
Toad-in-the-Hole with Chunky
Tomato Sauce 56
Tomato Sauce, Veal with 51
Tomatoes, Tuna-Stuffed 22
Tropical Kabobs 30

V

Veal with Tomato Sauce 51
Vegetable & Ham Quiche,
Spanish 47
Vegetables, Stir-Fried Beef & 74

W

Walnut Croquettes with
Watercress Dip, Cheese & 28
Watercress Dip, Cheese & Walnut
Croquettes with 28